Praise for *SwitchPoints*

No other serious book on leadership and change management has been able to so successfully combine organizational science, business, and good storytelling. The authors' use of data-driven science and real-life storytelling draws the reader into the fascinating world of railroads and the men and women who have such an impact on our lives. Down-to-earth examples compellingly highlight their fundamental ideas and principles.

SwitchPoints illustrates how to transform the culture of an organization and gain the much-needed organizational and people alignment essential to transforming a struggling or average company into a truly great and consistent performer.

Here are the tools, both credible and practical, that can focus a company's collective efforts by streamlining what is important: how to align people, priorities, and capital—an easy-to-understand common-sense approach to getting people to align actions and activities with a common set of goals.

> **—John W. Coyle, COO (retired), Trigon Healthcare Inc. and Aetna U.S. Healthcare**

Brilliant and thought-provoking. Best book I have read on how to change a company's culture and start tapping the talents of all your people. An organized and readable how-to manual with a practical approach. Filled with clarity and powerful insight.

> **—Jim Grossett, Senior Vice President of Human Resources, Agrium Inc.**

SwitchPoints requires little translation from railway stories to a large corporate arena. With different process challenges and similar people issues, effecting and sustaining behavior change is the most difficult thing we face as leaders. CN and CLG share the nuts-and-bolts tools used to turn a struggling enterprise into an industry leader. Be prepared to update your current business plan with ideas, tools, and methodologies proven in *SwitchPoints*.

> **—Capabilities Director, Fortune 100 Financial Services Company**

SwitchPoints delivers a compelling story of the value of doing all the basics really well, and by doing so, achieving extraordinary success—for shareholders, customers, and employees.

The book delivers excellent lessons on how to engage employees in total alignment with a company's mission, how to train them, stay the course—and in doing all of these things, achieve noteworthy success in distancing CN from its competitors. It's an easy read, blending personal anecdotes with good academic theory, and grounded in commercial reality.

Well done—congratulations to CN, to Hunter Harrison, its steadfast CEO leader, and to the authors. There is something in *SwitchPoints* for everyone—from people starting careers all the way to veteran executives. A great story!

> **—Doug Tough, CEO, Ansell Healthcare LTD**

A road map to achieving enhanced results for shareholders—and employees. The power of the ABCs [behavioral science] is made clear through specific examples. This book will help you analyze your situation by closely examining the secrets of a tremendous success story. It's a must-read for leaders who desire a high-performing team like no other!

> **—Michael D'Ambrose, Senior Vice President, HR, Archer Daniels Midland Company**

Through the powerful story of CN, *SwitchPoints* offers a valuable point of reference for all leaders who are working in an environment that is experiencing or is in need of change. I have found myself revisiting the various models outlined and applying them to current issues I was dealing with in my organization—a clear sign to me that this book makes an impact. Regardless of the industry you work in, I highly recommend it.

—John Silverthorn, Senior Vice President, Human Resources

Any leader who longs to transform the organization from a low-performance culture to a high-performance culture should pay close attention to the lessons of CN's transformation, as told in this book. CN achieved spectacular results from its frontline workforce, not by inventing new ideas, but by brilliantly executing the fundamentals we are all familiar with. It focused the behavioral change directly on measurable business results. It invested thousands of hours of hands-on coaching to help frontline supervisors become better performance managers. And it harnessed the sustained commitment from the CEO and other senior leaders. *SwitchPoints* tells a rare and compelling story of a company that really did it.

—Helen Handfield-Jones, President, Handfield Jones Inc.

SwitchPoints captures the leadership philosophy of CN's dynamic CEO, Hunter Harrison, and the approach his team employed to engineer one of the most successful corporate turnarounds in recent history. Few believed CN could survive, much less become a thriving, world-class example of best-in-class practices across business disciplines. Hunter quarterbacked the team, which built and sustains a successful business enterprise, practices corporate responsibility with diligence, and respects employees and partners while never losing sight of customers.

Every organization and corporate executive can benefit from the principles, practices, and lessons contained in *SwitchPoints*. The LPGA's course, which includes substantial business model and organizational change, is clearly benefiting from the CN journey and the example it teaches.

—Carolyn F. Bivens, Commissioner,
Ladies Professional Golf Association

This is a book about a great railroader, Hunter Harrison, and the incredible results he and his team have achieved at CN. It is about a largely self-educated man who has been a continuous learner all his life. Hunter thinks outside the box and has a charismatic personality and good judgment. Most business leaders talk about the importance of people, but as this book illustrates, Hunter lives and breathes it, and the rewards from such a commitment to people are obvious at CN.

Hunter developed Five Guiding Principles which became the major component of CN's strategy. The fifth Guiding Principle is people, and Hunter is of the view that if you get the people thing right, the first four Guiding Principles look after themselves. If you want to see the importance of having easily understood strategies and an incredible ability to execute, read this book.

—Purdy Crawford, C.C., Osler, Hoskin & Harcourt

This eye-opening book puts you into the vision and work being done at CN. I could relate to their vision, issues, and concerns while applying their techniques to my own environment and culture.

You can feel the engagement of the people and understand how the foundation was being built. It shows the real-life experiences, risk-taking, leadership, and vision being pulled together to satisfy the customer and grow the business. Most books tell what was done and recommend what you need to do, then leave you hanging. This book does not do that. It offers the tools used to achieve success. This book can be understood by and be helpful at every level in an organization.

—**Gary Cook, Facility Leader, Owens Corning Glass Metal Services**

I found this book refreshing and thought-provoking. *SwitchPoints* will help me become a better leader.

—**Dean Moll, Vice President, Continuous Improvement,
Pepperidge Farm, Incorporated**

We have all admired the revolutionary speed with which CN has become a legend in the industry, and wondered just how this achievement was realized. *SwitchPoints* provides the answer. It also provides a blueprint for other organizations to follow. In true Hunter Harrison fashion, *SwitchPoints* describes the arcane use of behavioral science tools with fascinating and inspirational stories. Anyone who reads *SwitchPoints* and is not motivated to apply the same principles to their own organization has jumped the switch.

—**Don Krusel, President & CEO, Prince Rupert Port Authority**

In addition to tracing the near-term evolution of what arguably is the best-run railroad in North America, *SwitchPoints* serves as a primer for propagating culture change in the far-flung, steeped-in-history environment that is this thing called railroading. But you don't have to be a railroader to reap what this book sows. The story is supported by data and case study–like anecdotes detailing the enlightened journeys that various CN managers and employees have taken during the past few years. And it is sprinkled with drop-dead candor from CEO Hunter Harrison. *SwitchPoints* is a blueprint for would-be change agents at organizations of any size or ilk. It's a living, breathing benchmarking tool that strategic thinkers can use as they attempt to chart their own continuous improvement courses.

—**Pat Foran, Editor in Chief, *Progressive Railroading* Magazine**

So many important themes and ideas in one small package! It is not easy to change the direction of an enterprise, especially one where the existing ways of operating are so deeply engrained. CN has succeeded in an arena where most fail. "If you accept what you believe to be your limitations, you'll never become better." If you want to improve, and succeed with dramatic change, read this book!

—**Paul Juniper, Director, Industrial Relations Centre, Queen's University**

Change is the only constant in today's business environment. This fact, while readily accepted by leaders, often results in poorly conceived and executed change initiatives—leading to a frenzy of debilitating organizational activities. *SwitchPoints* is a fascinating story of the opposite—an inspiring success story. It is a powerful documentation of successful culture change on the fast track as CN moves on a journey from a grand old railroad Crown Corporation, with all its entitlements to a publicly owned company requiring rigorous business acumen and laser-focused performance. This in-depth account of CN's journey will be immensely valuable to corporate leaders facing the change challenge.

—**Dr. Anne Golden, C.M., President and Chief Executive Officer,
The Conference Board of Canada**

Many talk about changing culture or transformation, but few actually do it. *SwitchPoints* is an outstanding chronology of how CN fundamentally transformed itself. More than a case study, it is based on pragmatic principles for sustained change. These ideas can be adapted to any executive wanting to shift employees from cynicism to commitment. It shifts culture change from academic ideas to concrete behaviors. It will return far more than the 2:1 results improvement it advocates.

—Dave Ulrich, Professor, University of Michigan Ross School of Business, and Partner, The RBL Group

SwitchPoints details the transformation of a stodgy, government-owned railroad from a perennial poor performer nicknamed "The Pig" to one of North America's most efficient, well-run businesses.

The book highlights the importance of having a leader who understands the contribution of operations to the success of any railroad. Hunter truly knows the railroad business, having begun his career in an entry-level position as a teenager and working his way through almost every position and level of management in the industry.

Hunter was aided by a human resources department and a consulting group that helped implement his vision across their system. His vision is that everyone in the company should understand the importance of operations. The company's financial results reflect that vision.

SwitchPoints encapsulates one of the great turnaround stories, not only of the railroad business, but in all of North American business.

—Dick Davidson, Chairman (retired), Union Pacific Railroad Company

SwitchPoints stands as a testament to the commitment of Hunter Harrison to maintain CN as a premier transportation company.

The book provides insights into his straightforward approach to being an agent of change, adapting principles of behavioral science to real life inside the rail industry. Methods to drive change such as the "ABC" approach are well illustrated, and business leaders may be intrigued by the Consequence Pyramid.

The change of culture within CN—through leadership training, employee development at all levels, and measurement feedback—makes for a worthwhile read.

—Kelley Anderson, UPS Corporate Transportation

I enjoyed reading *SwitchPoints*. The book reminded me of my first meeting with Hunter, which almost turned into a fight. Hunter turned out to be a straight-talking, sincere man. We are both passionate about safety and training—he gave me his word to fix many of the issues we raised, and he delivered. Our respective teams have worked hard to do the right things for CN and our members, including resolving long-festering issues. When leaders decide to work together for a common good, it is a powerful combination. It starts with mutual respect and integrity. We took the first important steps at that first meeting.

—Leo Gerard, International President, United Steelworkers Union

The book is absolutely practical, full of examples. It is a testament to all the best practices from CLG. Its content applies to any business in any sector.

—Stéphane Boisvert, President, Enterprise Group, Bell Canada

SwitchPoints

CULTURE CHANGE ON THE FAST TRACK
FOR BUSINESS SUCCESS

Judy Johnson, PhD

Les Dakens

Peter Edwards

Ned Morse

WILEY

John Wiley & Sons, Inc.

Copyright © 2008 by The Continuous Learning Group, Inc. (CLG). All rights reserved.

Published by John Wiley & Sons, Inc., Hoboken, New Jersey.
Published simultaneously in Canada.

No part of this publication may be reproduced, stored in a retrieval system, or transmitted in any form or by any means, electronic, mechanical, photocopying, recording, scanning, or otherwise, except as permitted under Section 107 or 108 of the 1976 United States Copyright Act, without either the prior written permission of the Publisher, or authorization through payment of the appropriate per-copy fee to the Copyright Clearance Center, Inc., 222 Rosewood Drive, Danvers, MA 01923, (978) 750-8400, fax (978) 750-4470, or on the web at www.copyright.com. Requests to the Publisher for permission should be addressed to the Permissions Department, John Wiley & Sons, Inc., 111 River Street, Hoboken, NJ 07030, (201) 748-6011, fax (201) 748-6008, or online at http://www.wiley.com/go/permissions.

Limit of Liability/Disclaimer of Warranty: While the publisher and author have used their best efforts in preparing this book, they make no representations or warranties with respect to the accuracy or completeness of the contents of this book and specifically disclaim any implied warranties of merchantability or fitness for a particular purpose. No warranty may be created or extended by sales representatives or written sales materials. The advice and strategies contained herein may not be suitable for your situation. You should consult with a professional where appropriate. Neither the publisher nor author shall be liable for any loss of profit or any other commercial damages, including but not limited to special, incidental, consequential, or other damages.

For general information on our other products and services or for technical support, please contact our Customer Care Department within the United States at (800) 762-2974, outside the United States at (317) 572-3993 or fax (317) 572-4002.

Wiley also publishes its books in a variety of electronic formats. Some content that appears in print may not be available in electronic books. For more information about Wiley products, visit our web site at www.wiley.com.

The following are registered trademarks or service marks of The Continuous Learning Group, Inc. For information and permissions, please contact Intellectual Property Manager, CLG, 500 Cherrington Corporate Center, Suite 350, Pittsburgh, PA 15108, www.clg.com.

- Consequence Pyramid[SM]
- DCOM® Model
- E-TIP Analysis[SM]
- Discretionary Performance[SM]
- Fluency Model[SM]
- Q4 Leadership[SM] Model
- SaFE[SM] Curve

Library of Congress Cataloging-in-Publication Data:
Switchpoints : culture change on the fast track for business success / Judy Johnson . . . [et al.].
    p. cm.
    Includes index.
    ISBN 978-0-470-28383-7 (cloth)
  1. Canadian National Railways—History.   2. Railroads—Canada—History.   I. Johnson, Judy, 1971–
    HE2810.C14S95 2008
    385.065'71—dc22
                                       2008022841

Printed in the United States of America

10 9 8 7 6 5 4 3 2 1

We dedicate this book to E. Hunter Harrison, the dynamic, visionary, get-it-done CEO who has revolutionized the Canadian National Railway Company.

From his early days as a Memphis teenager who oiled bearings on railcars, up through the ranks at Frisco, Burlington Northern, and Illinois Central, to the helm at CN, Hunter Harrison has proven himself a mighty diesel who runs on arrow-straight track, propelling CN to the top of the industry.

Like Henry Ford, who actually knew how to build cars, Hunter knows how to assemble trains, repair cars and track, and schedule shipments. He is the father of Precision Railroading, an operating philosophy that is spreading from CN to competing railways. Simply put: Hunter Harrison knows how to run a railroad.

Hunter possesses that magical combination of decisiveness, ability to execute, tough but compassionate personality, and just plain charisma that has forged him into a powerful leader. He is aggressive yet open to feedback and is a continuous learner.

Hunter's legendary people-focus has made him a leader who believes in his team—managers, staff, and unionized employees alike. He phones employees clear down to the front line at will, perhaps to ask about a family situation, or to thank a supervisor for going way over his numbers—or to demand a good reason why locomotive 5620 has been sitting motionless for two hours in the rail yard.

Common sense permeates Hunter's style. He thinks hard, explains his strategy to his team, and then does what works. He is intensely process-oriented, knowing that the right processes make things run right. He thinks big and drills down to where the wheels meet the rails.

Hunter also learned early that processes don't work right unless the people do. He knows that successful operations are all about behavior. That's why he enlisted behavioral scientists to help him drive CN's amazing performance.

Hunter did not start out to be an educator or author, but he has become both. To share his railroading knowledge and leadership fluency, he created CN's Five Guiding Principles, Hunter Camps (leadership training), Railroader Certification, and the Railroad MBA. He freely shares his know-how with other CEOs and even competitors, both personally and through his books, How We Work and Why *and* Change, Leadership, Mud and Why.

Former Morgan Stanley Dean Witter railroad analyst James Valentine called him the "dean of railroading." Hunter is simply the finest railroader in the business today.

Contents

List of Illustrations

Foreword

We are at the dawn of a new Golden Age of Rail.

If you don't believe that, you are not looking at the evidence. In today's climate of change, the trucking industry struggles with fuel cost, clogged highways, and decaying infrastructure. Airlines are failing and reducing service, for many reasons. And planet-wide, we have financial markets in deep trouble, political instability that threatens our oil economy, and the whole global warming/pollution mess.

Amidst this gloom, a winner is quietly emerging: our fuel-efficient, economical, low-polluting, dependable railroads. A current ad campaign claims that rail can move a ton of freight over 400 miles on a single gallon of diesel, and that is not advertising puff: it is true.

The coming decade will be transformative. We will enjoy a virtual explosion of rail transport.

No railway is better-positioned for this than Canadian National Railway.

Among my life's most gratifying experiences has been my involvement with CN as the railroad grew from a bureaucratic, inefficient government-owned operation to become the international transportation phenomenon we call "North America's Railway."

I saw CN privatized with its IPO in 1995. I watched CN's leadership trim the fat, dramatically cut cost, and expand through the United States and into Mexico, becoming the first major NAFTA railway. I watched CN's management excel, making the railroad number one among the Big Six railways on our continent.

I've had the pleasure of working with CN's top leaders—pragmatic visionaries like Paul Tellier, Michael Sabia, Hunter Harrison, Claude Mongeau, Jim Foote, and many others—to shape the railroad's financial success and status as a première investment (Bill Gates' investment entity is currently CN's largest shareholder).

It is these leaders who have positioned CN to lead the pack as the rail revival spreads across North America.

This book, *SwitchPoints,* tells the story of CN's remarkable climb to number one, achieved under the command of a truly great rail-roader, Hunter Harrison.

Hunter is a largely self-educated dynamo. He has been a continuous learner all his life, thinking outside the box. Hunter is famous for his charismatic personality, judgment, fairness, and toughness. Nobody executes strategy like Hunter Harrison, who is noted for calling anyone in the company, top to bottom, to praise a good performance, to ask how someone's surgery went, or to ask why a train is sitting idle (he monitors all of them from his office).

Hunter created Precision Railroading, the simple concept of focusing on getting customer's products delivered reliably, as opposed to just running trains efficiently. As Hunter says, Precision Railroading is not a set of rules, but a new way of thinking—and that's exactly what Hunter has brought to CN throughout his tenure.

He also devised CN's Five Guiding Principles, which became the core of CN's operating strategy. The principles are Service, Cost Control, Asset Utilization, Safety, and People. Most business leaders talk about the importance of people, but Hunter actually lives and breathes that belief. Hunter says, "If you get the people Principle right, the other four Guiding Principles look after themselves."

Like Hunter, I am a great believer in building the quality of people, and that is really the central theme of this book. It is no accident that the authors are all "people experts." Two are Human Resources and Labor Relations visionaries—Les Dakens and Peter Edwards of CN. The other two are noted behavioral scientists from the Continuous Learning Group (CLG)—Judy Johnson and Ned Morse.

SwitchPoints reveals *how* CN transformed itself from good to great, employing Behavioral Science—that most valuable of "people technologies." The world's top-performing companies are rapidly recognizing that Behavioral Science is the crucial missing piece in executing strategy. Great strategy is essential, but if you can't get people to do what's required, your strategy will falter or fail. Behavioral Science to the rescue.

SwitchPoints abounds in lessons learned that can be applied to any company, any business, anywhere, because it is all about getting people to perform better to meet the organization's targets. *SwitchPoints* shows specific models, tools, and coaching methods that CLG used to help CN's leadership lead better.

Just as the lessons learned in this book have been priceless to Canadian National Railway, so will they be for the whole rail industry as the railroad revolution proceeds over coming decades. And the best news of all for readers of this book: the lessons learned and tools in *SwitchPoints* will be priceless to any company that needs to transform its culture, improve union relations, and build a workforce of stars.

—Purdy Crawford, C.C.
Osler, Hoskin & Harcourt LLP
Toronto

Mr. Crawford is a former corporate CEO and Chairman, a university Governor and Chancellor, and sits on the boards of several companies. He joined the board of CN leading up to its privatization and retired at the Annual Meeting in 2007. He is a Companion of the Order of Canada, the nation's highest honor.

Preface

This book is a story of hard-earned success, achieved through culture change, using the advanced techniques of applied behavioral science, and driven by remarkable leadership.

It is about Canadian National Railway Company (CN), which in 1995 went public after decades of government ownership, and executed a spectacular transformation from good to great, becoming known as "North America's Railroad."

This was achieved in a few short years in a company with 22,500 employees, 80 percent unionized, and spread from the Atlantic to the Pacific Oceans and the Gulf Coast.

The railway's uncommon leadership executed this transformation—not flawlessly, yet spectacularly well—with the guidance of CLG, a behavioral science consultancy.

To quote from a 2008 interview with Warren Buffet (not a shareholder):

> Mr. Buffett has been buying railroad stocks in recent years but said the market has probably recognized their value now. He was particularly impressed with Canadian National Railway.
>
> "You've got some good railways," he said. "Canadian National probably has the best record of any railroad I know of. . . .
>
> "My friend Bill Gates bought a lot of that [CN], but he's smarter than me."[1]

Like all railroads, CN developed historically as a mostly male culture. Part of our culture change has been the extensive hiring of women in jobs throughout the workforce. However, in this book we elected not to use the awkward generics "he/she" and "him/her," but instead to use the simple pronoun "he" to be understood as a generic form to reference a person of either sex. We hope our readers understand and accept this usage.

Getting the Most from This Book

SwitchPoints is about one of the world's most successful railroads, Canadian National Railway. The company was at the top of its industry, but the leadership knew they couldn't rest. To stay number one, they had to fundamentally change its culture. This meant changing peoples' behavior.

This book tells the inspiring story of successes and failures. It describes the lessons we learned and the powerful behavioral tools we used. But this story's lessons don't just apply to a unionized railroad! They are valid for *any organization at any stage of success and to leaders who care about making a difference.*

- If you are in a nonindustrial business, what worked here can work for you, too—because behavioral tools work anywhere. You will find the leadership practices used here are directly applicable to any business. In Part VI: Assessing Switchpoints' Impact, we share stories from our corporate offices.
- If your company has a different culture from the story presented here, that just means differences in *how* you use the information in this book. Behavioral tools apply in any culture, country, or industry worldwide.
- What if you are seeking tools to help with your team instead of the entire organization? We provide many examples of what key leaders can do at the team level. The most influential person for an employee is his manager. As a leader, you can do a lot to improve the environment for those who work on your team.
- Looking to change the world? Then read this book cover to cover! We've put in our learnings—successes and failures both—to help you benefit from our efforts.

SwitchPoints is meant to be read as a story, so sit back and enjoy. This book offers plenty of inspiration, takeaways, and stories to excite any leader, executive, manager, business reader, or rail buff.

We hope you enjoy it, and invite you to read more of our story at www.switchpointsbook.com.

Judy Johnson
Les Dakens
Peter Edwards
Ned Morse

Acknowledgments

It does not take a village to write a book—it takes two companies! The richness of *SwitchPoints* comes from the collective expertise of CN in the business of rail transportation and CLG in the business of applying the tools of behavioral science to improve business performance, all distilled by our quartet of authors into the story told here.

Collectively, the authors wish to acknowledge the invaluable contributions of our editor, Fred Schroyer. Throughout the process, Fred was a consistent, unflappable force of knowledge, experience, and encouragement. He shared his experience freely, was always a joy to work with, and a professional in navigating all the ups and downs of the publishing process.

Thank you also to our Executive Editor at Wiley, Debra Englander. Her unwavering support and commitment to this book were critical to its publication. We also thank the production people at Wiley for their fine work and focus on quality.

Julie Moore, our project coordinator, was instrumental in managing all the details, as well as managing the efforts of many others who worked on the production team. Special thanks go to Janet Coen for keeping every draft in top shape and her hawk-eyed proofreading.

There are so many others who helped in telling their stories and in producing the book, we cannot possibly name them all. Thank you to everyone who has been involved in the development of this book—we couldn't have done it without you!

Individually, the authors wish to acknowledge those who helped them create *SwitchPoints*.

Judy Johnson: SwitchPoints was made possible by the countless efforts of hundreds of CN leaders and over twenty CLG consultants to bring about the change described in the book. While we share many stories in *SwitchPoints,* they are only a few of the many, many stories that make up the fabric of the culture of CN.

I want to acknowledge all of the efforts of the many CLG consultants and the support team who have played a role in helping CN tap and leverage their strengths. The team includes Lee Berti, Judy Bohannon, Paula Butte, Brenda Chartrand, Marcia Corbett, George Greanias, Bruce Hamilton, Jack Hinzman, Lois Hogan, Vince Johnson, Catherine Johnston, Will Jones, Donna Kullman, Jean-Yves Lord, Travis McNeal, Jacques Michaud, Julie Moore, Sherry Perkins, Steve Quesnelle, Galen Reese, Jerry Remillard, Russ Ridley, Richard Sandrock, Susan Shaw, Carol Smith, and Bob Vaughan.

Thank you also to my coauthors Les Dakens, Ned Morse, and Peter Edwards. This book is a product of the creativity and partnership we share, and would not have happened without our combined efforts. I am appreciative of everyone at CLG who helped select the stories, review the book, and give the support needed for us to bring it to life. Thanks particularly to Julie Smith for sharing her time and expertise in helping us shape the final product.

And finally, I thank my friends and family who have lived and breathed the development of this book with me. My husband Rob and our children Lena and Smith have shown unwavering support throughout the process. From my writing during family trips and vacations, to weekend reviews, and inconvenient deadlines—they have graciously supported all of it.

Les Dakens: I thank my CEO, Hunter Harrison, for his unwavering support of me and my team. As I wrap up my career and prepare to move on to the next phase of my life, I'm proud to say that it's a great way to finish my career: in my best job with my best boss. And I thank former CEO Paul Tellier for hiring me in the first place, and giving me the opportunity of my career.

I'm grateful to my CLG coauthors Ned Morse and Judy Johnson for the great trust they have built within CN and for their extraordinary working styles. To my talented spouse and writer, Marijane Dakens, I offer deep thanks for assistance in drafting my chapters.

To my Human Resources/Labor Relations team, the best in the business, thank you. And to my coauthor Peter Edwards, a great concept guy who will be running his own shop one of these days—profound thanks.

My thanks to Kim Madigan for her leadership of the Labour Relations function at CN.

And finally, thank you, CN leaders and employees—you are the reason for the People Department.

Peter Edwards: If you see my name and say, "I know that guy," then thank you—you are part of any achievement that is here. I have learned continuously from so many brilliant and thoughtful people in my career that you should all share in the credit.

There are a few who must be mentioned specifically. I'll begin with Dr. Pradeep Kumar and Dr. Don Wood, my professors at Queen's, who introduced me to the worlds of HR and LR. I would not be doing what I do today without their intervention at a critical juncture.

To CEO Hunter Harrison and my coauthor Les Dakens—I could not have asked for two more passionate thinkers and doers on people and leadership. Gentlemen, you have been inspirational. Thanks to my team at CN, you have suffered through many of my dreams and made them even more than I dared hope.

To my parents and brothers and sister—thank you for your love and support for these many years and the multitude of things I have learned from you. If you want to understand people dynamics, come from a big family.

And finally, to my wife Maxine and my boys Noah and Luke— I have spent a lot of time traveling and writing in the past few years, but there was never a moment that you were not in my thoughts and in my heart.

Ned Morse: This work would not have been possible without the vision and trust of my coauthors Peter Edwards and Les Dakens, and the support of CEO Hunter Harrison and executives Claude Mongeau, Gordon Trafton, and Keith Creel. Nor could this book have happened without the passion of key CLG colleagues—George Greanias in the early days, then Galen Reese, and most recently my coauthor Judy Johnson. Each led the teams of dedicated, results-focused, hard-working CLG consultants and CN personnel who teamed to make CN's culture changes real.

The approaches undergirding this change effort were born in the delight of my career-long collaboration with Jim Hillgren and honed through the interaction with the many consultants and clients I've been fortunate to work alongside over these past 30 years. My own effectiveness is due largely to the tireless patience of my executive assistant Judy Bohannon, who has kept me on track for 18 years now.

And at the core, my ability to contribute to this amazing change in CN's corporate culture could not have been possible without the support of my long-suffering, never-complaining wife Vicki and our children David, James, William, and Mary Elizabeth. You all have experienced my being gone almost more than I've been home—but you have never been out of my thoughts.

Introduction:
A Broken Culture

How broken can a corporate culture get? E. Hunter Harrison, CEO of Canadian National Railway (CN), shares a moment of truth:

> I was touring some of our properties. I visited a terminal and discovered a puzzling problem.
>
> After a few hours of walking around, I saw that something was terribly wrong. *The people were missing.*
>
> I pumped managers to find out what was going on. Finally they admitted they were letting employees go home early—four hours early, every day—yet paying them for a full eight hours. I was shocked. "That has to stop today," I told them, and started to walk away.
>
> Then a supervisor approached me. "Mr. Harrison," he said quietly, "it's worse than this at the other terminals."
>
> "Where?" I asked.
>
> "Everywhere!"
>
> Our railway had been a Canadian government agency for decades, and had been sold to investors only four years earlier. If we were to succeed as a private company, we had to act fast on these "early quits," as they were called. "Stop it now. Today!" I was growing passionate, my voice rising.
>
> "Stop it where?"
>
> "Everywhere, of course!"
>
> "Okay, we'll stop it *almost* everywhere . . . except in Western Canada."
>
> "Why not there?" I demanded.
>
> "Because those cowboys will shut us down."
>
> "Then start with them."

"What?!"

"I said, start with them. If we are going to have a @#&*! match over this, we might as well start in the toughest place!"

It absolutely amazed me that we could have a dispute over asking people to work the hours we pay them for! But that is how broken cultures can get.

**(Adapted with permission from
E. Hunter Harrison,
Change, Leadership, Mud and Why, © 2008
Canadian National Railway Company)**

You might think this story came from a struggling company that was barely scraping by, but that couldn't be further from the truth. At the time of this story, CN was at the top of its industry. It was the number one railroad, beating the competition at every turn. Obviously, there was still room for improvement.

The Culture of Early Quits

CN wasn't the only railway that tolerated what are called "early quits." Other railroads across North America had negotiated six hours of work for eight hours of pay. Unlike the other railroads, though, CN hadn't *negotiated* reduced work hours—supervisors just *granted* them, in the hope that extra hours off would motivate employees to work harder and move trains faster.

That was the kind of thinking that needed to change. It was the culture that CN's leadership was up against. In the complex orchestration of a modern railroad, every employee counts, every day. Railroading is a tough business that demands a conscientious contribution from every employee, whether he drives, repairs, schedules, manages, inspects, or bills. The railway counted on everyone being there, head in the game, every day.

Early quits meant that the employees only finished half the job. This practice supported putting in your time rather than getting the job done. No company can survive that way for long.

Even worse, look at the message it sent to employees. Allowing early quits implied that employees weren't really needed for half of each day, and therefore must not have been adding value. What would that indifference tell you about your importance to your own company?

Of course, the truth was that CN cared deeply about its employees. Ironically, managers had allowed early quits because they thought that would demonstrate how much they cared. Little did they realize that it demonstrated just the opposite.

A New Trip Plan

Despite CN's success, this moment highlighted the need to go much further, to fix the culture that had developed over time. This moment revealed the future, and Hunter Harrison knew that if he and his leadership team did not correct the culture soon, CN would not remain the industry leader.

Without change, CN would slowly slip back. It would have to work hard to maintain momentum while the competition continued to improve. CN could be the best forever only if everyone in the company knew the goals, knew his part, and was committed to the collective success. That required more than just change—it required massive, organization-wide *culture change.*

On the railway, any number of tracks can get you from Memphis to Vancouver, but there is one best way. That one best way is mapped out in what is called a *trip plan*. The trip plan shows the way to get to the destination with the lowest cost, shortest distance, fastest time, and the least risk of delay. It is the one route that offers the unique combination of features that enables moving rapidly, efficiently, reliably, and precisely from where you are now to where you want to be.

CN needed to find the right route to change the culture, and then set a trip plan to get there.

Switchpoints

On the railroad, every trip plan has points along the way where trains are switched from one track to another to ensure that they take the best route. These points are called *switchpoints*.

A switchpoint is where railroad tracks diverge, going in different directions. A mechanical switch sends a train in either direction A or B. Thus, a switchpoint is a very definite decision point that is managed to determine a train's destination. (See Figure I.1.)

Figure I.1   A Railroad Switchpoint

Source: Hunter Harrison, *How We Work and Why,* p. 134, © 2005 Canadian National Railway Company.

Switchpoints are part of every train's trip plan. The plan shows how switches need to be set to ensure that goods travel down the right track.

Let's say you want to ship 50 railcars of lumber from Prince George, British Columbia, to Memphis, Tennessee. The trip plan defines the critical decisions about direction—the switchpoints— necessary for the train to arrive in the right place on time. Operators manage each switchpoint, lining the switches to route the train in the right direction. Each switchpoint must be managed carefully, or that load of lumber might end up in Omaha or New Orleans.

Just as with a moving train, the route to culture change has many switchpoints along the way—points where decisions create watershed change for the organization and define its future. On a corporate scale, decisions that CN's leaders made at critical switchpoints were key to the railroad's survival and success. The choices made at these switchpoints determined the company's destination as the culture changed.

Looking back, some of the switchpoints in CN's culture change seem obvious now. Stopping early quits was a switchpoint with deep significance for the organization. Other switchpoints were less obvious, but equally significant—such as ensuring everyone was "dressed and ready" at the start of a shift, managing meeting effectiveness, and ensuring that every employee received feedback on his performance on a regular basis.

Since CN had become investor-owned, it had to create value for shareholders. CN could not afford to keep lumbering down the same old track. New switchpoints had to be identified and aligned to ensure the company's future.

Spiking the Switch

Not only did CN have to align switchpoints—leaders had to make sure there could be no return to the old ways. Railroaders have a term for that: *spiking the switch.*

Spiking the switch has a very powerful meaning to which every leader can relate. It literally means driving a heavy spike into a wooden railroad tie at a switchpoint to prevent the switch from moving. This keeps anyone from changing it back to the old direction. Railroaders spike the switch when a section of track is removed from service or when CN no longer delivers to a place. (See Figure I.2.)

Spiking the switch prevents trains from going the wrong way—permanently. In culture change, this means creating an environment where the company can't revert to its old ways.

In changing CN's culture, leaders often had to spike the switch for change, and then stay the course and be consistent. People could not be allowed the option of going back to the old way. Each switchpoint was an opportunity for leaders to align with the new direction, charge down the track, and sustain a new way of working.

Figure I.2   Railroad Spike
Source: Canadian National Railway Company.

By spiking the switches on practices that were no longer acceptable, CN strongly signaled the organization that the company's leaders were serious about changing the organization for the better. By spiking the switches, they showed they were not going back.

I

BUILDING ONE OF NORTH AMERICA'S TOP RAILROADS

Before we can tell you how CN achieved its culture change, you need to know the unique history of Canadian National Railway. Understanding this remarkable enterprise's 90-year history makes clear why we were so passionate about changing the company's culture.

CHAPTER 1

The Road to Best-in-Class

1830: Pioneering Days

Railroads in Canada began in the 1830s with one small rail line in Quebec, then expanded in a growing spiderweb from coast to coast. Like the transcontinental railroad that tied the United States together with its first coast-to-coast transportation link in 1869, the numerous Canadian rail lines networked together to achieve the same for Canada. (See Table 1.1.)

Railroads were the tech bubble of their day. The industry was chaotic, with startups and failures, mergers, and lack of standards. There were problems with interconnecting the rail lines of different companies—some used different spacing between their rails, so trains could not move continuously from rail line to rail line, and cargo had to be transferred from one company's train to another's.

By World War I (1914–1918), many Canadian railroads were failing. This posed a serious threat to Canada's economy and the nation itself, because in those days no national highway system offered backup transportation if the railroads failed. National survival demanded action.

1919: Nationalization

Starting in 1919, the Canadian government formed a holding company for this mass of floundering rail lines. Assembling the vast network of individual railroads into a coherent system took several

Table 1.1   Canadian National Railway—Milestones on Our Trip Plan

Timeline	Major Changes to the Trip Plan
1832	**Pioneering Days:** Railroads grow with Canada.
1919	**Nationalization:** Canadian National Railway is formed, consolidating many railways into a regulated government agency with 100,000 employees.
1980s	**Deregulation:** Railway deregulation in Canada and the United States encourages mergers, acquisitions, and a new competitiveness.
1992	**Organizational Redesign:** Paul Tellier takes the reins at CN and restructures the organization and leadership to better focus on operating results.
1995	**Privatization:** CN goes public with Canada's largest IPO.
1998	**Precision Railroading:** COO Hunter Harrison brings precision railroading and the Five Guiding Principles to managing the business.
2003	**Culture Change on the Fast Track:** Hunter Harrison becomes CEO and decides to embed performance improvement across the company through a massive culture change effort.

Source: Developed with data from the Canadian National Railway Company website.

years. The result was CN, a rail system that spanned Canada from the Atlantic to the Pacific. It served communities large and small, and became the national pride of Canada.

CN also became a major national employer, with over 100,000 on the payroll at its peak. This included not only the rail system, but subsidiary telephone companies (to support rail communications), hotels (to support tourism), the beginning of an airline (Air Canada), and even the Canadian Broadcasting Corporation (started by CN to provide radio entertainment on long rail journeys). As the decades passed, CN became Canada's economic backbone, with the best rail infrastructure in North America. As a business, it carried a good balance of commodities: coal, fertilizer, grain, forest products, automobiles and parts, and intermodal containerized cargo.

In 1975, CN built the world's tallest freestanding structure at the time, the famous CN Tower in Toronto. A platform for railway communications and radio and TV broadcasting, the magnificent tower also proclaimed Canada's success in world business and industry.

The 1980s: Deregulation

Over time, the railroad had become a lot of things besides a national cargo hauler: hotelier, ferry service provider, truck line. One thing it wasn't was profitable.

In 1980, U.S. railroads were deregulated under the Staggers Act, freeing their operations to become more competitive. In Canada, the National Transportation Act (1987) and the Canada Transportation Act (1996) gave similar freedom to Canada's commercial railways. But CN was locked into antiquated rules and the politics of Canadian government ownership, making improvement extremely difficult.

Also during the 1980s, double-digit interest rates revolutionized how business looked at inventory. No longer could companies afford large stock reserves, so they maintained the smallest possible inventories. Just-in-time shipping stood the freight world on its head. Traditional railways weren't built for this, so the trucking industry boomed, cutting deeply into the freight business, especially CN's.

In 1986, CN's long-term debt exceeded $3.4 billion, and interest charges alone surpassed $1 million a day. The railroad was burdened with hundreds of miles of business track that went to specific customers and carried extremely low volume, but the government would not abandon it. One-third of the track carried less than 1 percent of the business. CN was profitable in some years, but those profits occurred mostly when the railroad could jettison little-used track or large numbers of employees.

All this forced CN to further commoditize the business, and lower prices followed. Year after year, this downward slide of price cuts became a necessary way to keep and attract customers. As the railway struggled to lower costs, it quickly became a burden on the taxpayers. But in the commodity business, cutting prices was the main way to beat the competition.

Canada's national dream had become a national nightmare. Taxpayers were bailing out CN decade after decade, to the tune of tens of billions of dollars. But CN's trains ran late and deliveries were undependable. Running 500-plus trains daily was inefficient, customers were fed up, and bankruptcy rumbled at the doorstep. CN's bloated facilities and payroll led the media to bestow an unflattering nickname, "The Pig."

The government and CN's management struggled to improve matters, with occasional success. Some operations were sold off and some track mileage reduced. The payroll shrank from 51,000 to 38,000. Yet in 1992, the company lost over $1 billion in eastern Canada alone.

1992: Organizational Redesign

Clearly, it was time for a big change. That change was Paul Tellier. In 1992, he took the reins as CEO of the floundering company. Tellier had been the head of the Canadian government bureaucracy under two prime ministers of different political parties. His role in running the administration of the government can best be described as a "CEO of civil servants."

He was indeed a consummate bureaucrat—but he had no railroad experience. Labor, railroaders, and the investment community rolled their eyes. Few could picture him revolutionizing CN into a viable business, much less making CN into North America's number one railroad.

On one count, they had a point: Tellier didn't know the old-fashioned way of running a railroad. But his years in politics made him a master at overcoming bureaucracy, and he could assimilate huge volumes of data and make quick, incisive decisions. Critics completely underestimated Tellier's intense, hard-driving leadership and two of his greatest skills: building a team and executing a plan.

On his very first workday as CEO, Tellier met with union leaders. "I wanted to tell them that I was taking them seriously, but that they should take me seriously, too, because I was determined to turn this place around."[1]

To do this, Tellier gathered around him an exceptional group of executives. They included Michael Sabia, a genius in finance; Jim Foote, an expert in investor relations who knew how to talk to the Street; Claude Mongeau, another finance expert of great intellectual horsepower and strategic insight; and others. Together, they markedly improved relations with shareholders, government, and the unions.

When Tellier took over in 1992, CN's operating ratio was a horrendous 97.1. This meant that CN was spending 97.1 cents for every dollar earned. This was no way to run a company. For CN, each 1 percent of operating ratio equated to approximately $40 million.

If there were ever to be a meaningful bottom line, things would have to change drastically.

People cautioned Tellier to make changes slowly; "over five years" would be a good time frame, they said. But this was the exact opposite of what Tellier had planned. He saw in CN a too-comfortable corporation. He wanted to instill a visceral sense of urgency.

From then on there would be disciplined focus and follow-up. Projects would not sit in limbo amid endless analysis. Decisions would be made, and the right people put in place to make them. So it began.

A Quick Change

Tellier and his team quickly focused on the core business and sold off nearly 9,000 miles of track—an astonishing one-third of the rail network. They also disposed of CN's nonrailroad assets, including a hotel in Paris and the CN Tower. And they eliminated redundant processes that wasted time and money.

In less than four months, five senior executives were gone and not replaced. The entire CN payroll was cut by about one-third, including about 11,000 jobs over three years. Tellier reorganized his executive team and reduced management layers from as many as a dozen to only five between himself and the front line. He made it clear: Bureaucracy in CN was history, everyone must pull his own weight, and no one had guaranteed employment.

The sense of urgency and focus on the bottom line translated into immediate results. Within three years, the operating ratio dropped from the high 90s to the high 80s. CN's net income grew 3.5 times, from a loss in 1992 of $68 million to $204 million.

The results were impressive, but Tellier knew that long-term, bottom-line growth required more than just cost-cutting. He quickly turned his focus to the customer and new markets. He published a Customer Bill of Rights and a vision for the future.

The visionary Tellier correctly predicted the highly integrated role that railroads and trucking would share in freight handling that we see today. He foresaw the potential impact that the North American Free Trade Agreement (NAFTA) would have on an integrated North American economy. This NAFTA orientation was one that would shape the flow of sales, strategic acquisitions, and the destiny of Canadian National Railway for decades to come.

Table 1.2   CN's Financial Performance Impacted by Organizational Redesign (Canadian Dollars in Millions)

Year and Event	Operating Ratio (Adjusted)	Free Cash Flow	Revenue	Net Income (Adjusted)	Employees (End of Period)
1992 (Tellier arrives)	97.1%	$78	$3,897	$(68)	35,281
1995	89.0%	$118	$3,862	$204	23,999

Source: Adapted from financial data as disclosed in Canadian National Railway Company annual reports or publicly available data.

Tellier also prepared the company for the future by driving CN's technological advancement, including new infrastructure, remote-controlled locomotives, and computerized operations.

Viewing CN's business results, you can easily see the impact Tellier had on the company. (See Table 1.2.)

With the significant beginnings of a healthy bottom line, a new focus on the customer, and a company stoked for performance, it was time for the next phase.

1995: Privatization

Tellier's greatest accomplishment was the initial public offering in 1995 that privatized CN. At the time, it was the largest IPO in Canadian history. Some 83,800,000 shares went for over $2 billion on the stock exchanges in New York (CNI) and Toronto (CNR).

Overnight, the railroad went from government-owned to a publicly traded, investor-owned company. All of the employees were now working for the investors instead of the government.

Many thought the IPO would fail. But those who understood the strengths of CN, the rail industry and Tellier, knew it would succeed. However, it took great effort. To prime the investment community for the IPO, Tellier and others staged a memorable multimedia road show, hitting 26 cities in nine countries in only three weeks.[2]

In a stunning vote of confidence, over 11,000 CN employees, both unionized and nonunion, bought shares. This was the greatest employee shareholder percentage (over 40 percent) of any North American railroad.

Tellier's decade as CEO (1992–2002) transformed the railway from a money-loser to a much leaner, profitable, investor-owned corporation. The IPO was about much more than cash, however, as noted in a book that tells the IPO story, *The Pig That Flew.*

> Throughout CN, a competitive spirit took hold. Workers seemed proud to serve not a government bureaucracy, but a customer-driven, investor-driven railway. The privatization, Tellier says, had been "a tremendously powerful instrument in our transformation. Our people have become more bottom line–oriented. They want to see a higher share price and our performance improved." In short, the revolution in CN's corporate culture was well underway. Its rewards would soon prove dramatic.[3]

The Right Leaders for the Job

People talk about "the right man for the job," and Tellier was the right leader for his era of CN's history. He had skillfully led CN through two critical phases. The first was creating a sense of urgency and focus, revamping the bottom line, and reshaping customer relationships. The second phase, taking the railway public in a record-setting privatization, was followed by continued leaps in bottom-line performance. Those wise enough to see what was happening would be well rewarded for the CN shares they bought.

These two phases were transformational for CN, but Tellier was not done. He was building for the future with a strong executive team to lead the organization. In Tellier's own words:

> When I came to CN, I knew very little about railroads, but a lot about people. Over the years, I'd developed the skill of quickly figuring out who could make things happen. This was a critical skill for my early days at CN. If we were going to make the changes that were required, I knew that many managers had to be changed and new leaders brought in or moved up. . . .
>
> I was always looking for that future talent. I found a pool of it in a regional U.S. railroad known as Illinois Central. Its network was a perfect fit for our railroad and gave us the NAFTA penetration that I knew was critical for CN's future.

It also gave me access to some great railroaders, including Hunter Harrison [Illinois Central's president]. So when we put the deal together, I made sure that Hunter and his leadership team agreed to join the CN team. Retaining Hunter Harrison was probably one of the best decisions I took as CEO of CN.[4]

1998: Precision Railroading

In 1998, CN acquired the Illinois Central Railroad, with approval in 1999. Overnight, Canadian National Railway was converted from a mostly Canadian operation to "North America's Railroad." (See Figure 1.1.)

CN now spanned the continent from sea to sea, plus the Gulf Coast, with connections into Mexico via alliance partners. The result made CN a true NAFTA railway.

Along with the Illinois Central (IC), CN acquired something else that would revolutionize its future: IC's President Hunter Harrison, who became CN's new Chief Operating Officer (COO).

Harrison was the real thing, a true railroader. While still in high school, he had labored for a railroad in Memphis. Over the years, his leadership talent had emerged as he worked his way up in different railroads. At the Illinois Central, he had become renowned for his strong, action-oriented style. He was the right man to continue what Tellier had started.

When Harrison came on board as COO in 1998, he taught CN a new way of working—a better way of railroading. His vision was to make CN the best-performing, most profitable railroad on the planet.

Harrison made his vision clear through his *Five Guiding Principles,* principles that quickly became CN's core pillars against which every idea, plan, and action could be tested. At every opportunity, he talked with his leadership team, managers, and employees about the Five Guiding Principles: Service, Cost Control, Asset Utilization, Safety, and People.

Harrison built on the pillars of the Five Guiding Principles and broke with the prevailing way of running a railroad by next introducing *Precision Railroading.* Traditionally, rail carriers would hold a train until it was completely full before departing. This maximized efficiency for the railroad, but could delay an individual customer's shipments, sometimes by days. This would be

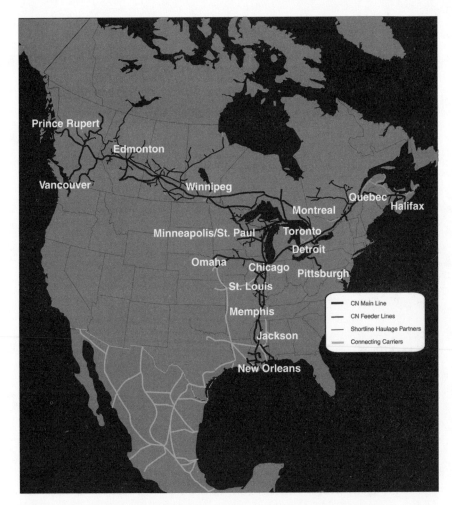

Figure 1.1   CN Rail System Map: "North America's Railroad"
Source: Canadian National Railway Company.

equivalent to holding a flight until every seat is taken, making the plane late and delaying every passenger—efficient for the airline to fully utilize its asset, but problematic in disrupting the plans of unhappy passengers.

Traditional railroading gets full trains from A to B. Precision Railroading, by contrast, focuses on how to get *an individual customer's shipment* from A to B as quickly as possible, not the whole train. Accomplishing this makes it necessary to disassemble and reassemble trains as needed, transferring customers' railcars from train to train to keep them moving.

It is certainly a simple concept. But executing it takes dedication, planning, and vigorous leadership. Precision Railroading requires that every aspect of train operations—scheduling, locomotive availability, crew management, rail car repairs, track maintenance, and so on—be synchronized to keep individual customer railcars moving. No one wins when shipments are standing still.

Keeping shipments moving meant that managers constantly reviewed, revised, and adjusted each and every process related to customer delivery. It didn't take long for the discipline of Precision Railroading to permeate the entire organization, creating new value for CN's customers, value that competing rail carriers could not deliver.

The proof of Precision Railroading's value is compelling: In 1999, CN quoted a transit time of 7 to 9 days from Chicago to Edmonton (about 1,600 rail miles). Customers would ask, "Is it always between 7 and 9 days?" CN would say, "Well, sometimes 6 days, occasionally 10 or 11." This was a pretty typical railway offering—definitely not inspiring to shippers!

But Precision Railroading changed this. CN began quoting the trip in hours (which was 24 times more precise than quoting in days). Then leaders set a target: Accelerate the trip from 7 to 9 days (170 to 200 hours) to only 4.6 days (111 hours). At first, the results were shaky and inconsistent, as you would expect—the first few weeks, the 111-hour target was met only 48 percent of the time. But within four months, that rose to above 90 percent. Today, CN runs a train from Prince George in British Columbia to Chicago in less than 100 hours—which is an additional 500 miles, in less time, with greater reliability.

To make Precision Railroading work, every employee had to think differently. Instead of waiting for orders or for someone to solve a problem, it becomes each employee's responsibility to take initiative, demonstrate leadership, spot problems, and fix them. Leaders needed each employee to continually share knowledge and information, and to be aware that every action has a far-reaching impact on the operation. Local operations now had to think in terms of the entire network, not just their own piece of it.

Precision Railroading became a switchpoint for the organization. CN spiked the switch against traditional railroading—waiting for trains to be full. Henceforth, trains would arrive and depart on time and on schedule—full or not.

2003: Passing the Reins

The company's performance confirmed that it was heading down the right track. By January 2003, when Paul Tellier moved on and Hunter Harrison was elevated to CEO, the results of their teamwork were obvious to all. (See Table 1.3.)

Many years of hard work had paid off. By the end of 2002, CN not only had become North America's railroad, but North America's *top* railroad. Clearly, the leadership had made CN the strongest performer among the Big Six railways. Operating ratio dropped, freeing up profits to reinvest in the company. Revenue was almost double, and achieved by fewer employees.

CN's strong operating results drove equally strong stock performance on both U.S. and Canadian markets, as shown in Figure 1.2. Note the two highest curves in the figure.

Six years after the IPO, CN's stock under Tellier and Harrison generated the highest total shareholder return of any Class I railroad. (Currently, a Class I railroad is defined by the Association of American Railroads—AAR—as one with annual revenue exceeding $319.3 million.) To make this personally relevant: If you had

Table 1.3   CN's Financial Performance Impacted by Precision Railroading (Canadian Dollars in Millions)

Year and Event	Operating Ratio (Adjusted)	Free Cash Flow	Revenue	Net Income (Adjusted)	Employees (End of Period)
1995 (Privatization)	89.0%	$(118)	$3,862	$204	23,999
1998 (Harrison arrives: Precision Railroading begins)	75.3%	$228	$4,078	$569	19,198
End of 2002	70.5%	$513	$6,339	$1,052	22,114

Source: All financial data as disclosed in Canadian National Railway Company annual reports and/or Investor Factbooks. Adjusted to exclude items affecting comparability of results.

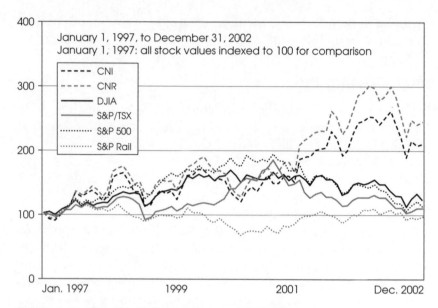

Figure 1.2   CN's Stock Performance, 1997–2002

Source: Adapted from financial data as disclosed in Canadian National Railway Company annual reports or publicly available data.

invested $70,000 in CN stock at the time of the IPO and reinvested the dividends, a decade later you would have earned close to $1 million. A number of CN employees did just that.

By the time Harrison took over as CEO in January 2003, he and Tellier had already taken CN to best-in-class. And the story wasn't over . . .

CHAPTER 2

Culture Change on the Fast Track

By 2002, CN was doing very well. But leaders struggled with a question: How can we take our company—now best-in-class—and not just make it better, but achieve unheard-of levels of performance year-over-year on aspects of our annual operating plan?

In January 2003, Hunter Harrison became CEO. Uncovering early quits had shocked him, and he knew the answer lay in creating deep and lasting culture change. Despite all the gains made through Precision Railroading, CN still had a culture of early quits, where large numbers of people were allowed the option of doing just enough to get by.

Harrison realized that the success of Precision Railroading was due to his personal leadership of the effort. So, to continue improvements, he needed to make a change. He needed the entire leadership team to create a culture where everyone came to work every day consumed with achieving new levels of performance.

Acquisitions

CN's leadership faced an additional challenge in creating a new culture. As they defined the culture needed to get results, they were still merging cultures from acquired railways:

- Illinois Central Railroad (IC)—acquired in 1998 (approved 1999) for U.S. $2.4 billion. Buying the IC added a connection from Chicago to New Orleans, dramatically expanding CN from a predominantly east-west Canadian rail line to a full-blown North American railway.

- Wisconsin Central (WC)—acquired in 2001 for U.S. $0.8 billion. The Wisconsin Central gave CN better access around the western Great Lakes, plus a connection from Chicago to western Canada. The deal included the largest British rail freight company: the English, Welsh, and Scottish Railway (subsequently sold in 2007).

CN had made significant progress in integrating the best from the cultures of the Illinois Central and the Wisconsin Central into CN, and sharing the best of CN with them. But there was much more to do, and this made the challenge harder, with two further acquisitions under consideration:

- BC Rail (British Columbia)—acquired in 2004 for U.S. $1 billion. This was Canada's third-largest rail line, another Crown Corporation that serviced the most challenging terrain in Canada. Acquiring it expanded CN's potential for trans-Pacific commerce.
- Great Lakes Transportation (GLT) rail and related holdings— ultimately acquired in 2003 for U.S. $380 million. Adding GLT allowed a more direct connection between the United States and western Canada.

Harrison and his team knew that, if done right, they could use these two additional acquisitions—and others to follow—as ways of reshaping *all* of CN's culture.

Buying Other Cultures

When you acquire another company, you get three things: its assets, its people, and its company culture. The culture is an expression of how a company's people interact with its assets, establishing strong customs over time.

Assets and people are the easy part. In railroading, you get miles of rails and bridges, rolling stock and locomotives, rail yards, control systems, a team of employees, and balance sheets. These are things you can easily inspect before you buy.

Culture is not so easy. With each acquisition came a new culture that was ingrained into the way people worked.

Each acquisition brought dramatic new reach and opportunities to CN, but it also brought challenges—foremost among them the integration of new culture.

The Challenge

Precision Railroading had raised CN to the top of the industry, but Harrison knew that competition was getting tougher each year. If CN were to remain the leader, the pace of change would have to accelerate. Otherwise, competitors would overtake the company and CN could kiss the number one slot good-bye. Falling from top status was definitely not an option after working so long and hard to achieve best-in-class.

Yet CN had no magic, unique technology with which to out-flank competitors. All railroad hardware—track, locomotives, rail-cars, control systems, communications, maintenance equipment—came from the same suppliers used by all railways. The CN difference had to go deeper: It had to be CN's employees and their performance.

After examining CN's culture with a critical eye, Harrison came to believe that the greatest gains in performance were ahead—clearly seen by Harrison and perhaps a handful of others. On the day when CN announced Tellier's departure and Harrison's promotion to CEO, CN's stock dropped 2 percent. Had investors known how much improvement Hunter would spearhead, it's likely that the stock value would have gone upward instead.

The Results

In fact, CN's stock took only a brief dip before climbing to new levels of performance—note the two highest curves in Figure 2.1.

Under Harrison, CN was not just maximizing stock perfor-mance. The company was also exceeding its metrics in all other key categories. Here are results for the entire year 2007, from CN's 2007 annual report:

- Free cash flow: $828 million
- Revenue: $7,897 million
- Net income: $2,158 million
- Operating ratio: 63.6

All of these improvements in performance were accomplished with roughly the same number of employees.

How were other railways doing by comparison? CN's competitors—the other five of the Big Six—are Burlington Northern Santa Fe (BNSF), Norfolk Southern (NS), Union Pacific (UP),

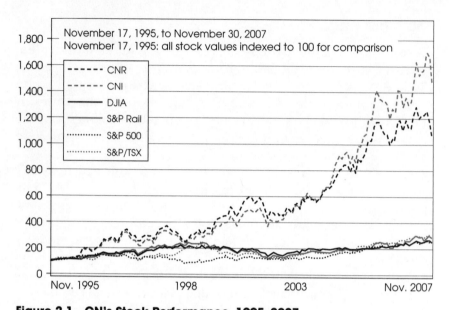

Figure 2.1 CN's Stock Performance, 1995–2007

Source: Adapted from financial data as disclosed in Canadian National Railway Company annual reports or publicly available data.

the former Chessie System (CSX), and Canadian Pacific (CP). CN's performance enabled the company to lead the industry in key metrics like operating ratio, which tells the story. While the operating ratio of CN's competitors stayed in the range of about 77 to 85 cents on the dollar, CN's steadily dropped from about 77 cents to 62 cents—proof that the hard work at culture change was paying off. (See Figure 2.2.)

As James Valentine, former Morgan Stanley Dean Witter Rail Analyst, noted: "CN is to freight railroading what Michael Jordan is to basketball and Tiger Woods is to golf."

The Trip Plan for Culture Change on the Fast Track

Even Tiger Woods has to have a game plan for his next big win. For CN, this meant setting the trip plan for culture change. So we created seven steps to take the company from its existing culture to a future culture of Discretionary Performance^{SM} and year-over-year improvements. The seven steps were:

1. *Clarify the vision.* We needed to ensure that everyone across the company understood the vision, the Five Guiding Principles,

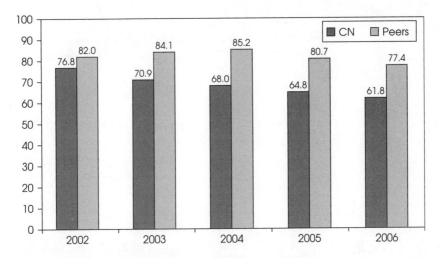

Figure 2.2   CN's Industry-Leading Operating Ratio
Source: Canadian National Railway Company 2007 annual report; other data from publicly available information and excludes CP.

and *how* we planned to get there by creating a new culture for the company.

2. *Choose the right switchpoints.* With the vision set and a clear understanding of our current culture, we needed to determine how to change that culture into one of an engaged, committed workforce. We needed to determine which switchpoints would set us on the right route to faster culture change.

3. *Select the tools for change.* On the railroad, the right tools make the difference in an employee's ability to complete a job safely and efficiently. In culture change, having the right tools has a similar impact—you need the right tools to ensure change. At CN, we found those tools in Behavioral Science.

4. *Align the switches.* With a clear vision of the culture we wanted to create, and the tools to do it right, we were ready to begin by aligning the switches in the right direction toward change. Aligning the switches required finding sponsorship, testing the business case for the tools, and setting a plan to broaden our efforts.

5. *Assess switchpoints' impact.* Once we had expanded the cultural change across the organization, we needed to track progress to determine if, in fact, we were on the right route.

Tracking progress was critical to ensuring that we had made the right decisions at key switchpoints. It also allowed us to demonstrate the value of the changes we were asking the organization to make.

6. *Spike the switches.* Through the process of changing the culture, we aligned several switchpoints, making decisions to move the company in a new direction, moving closer to our desired future state. For each of those decisions, we needed to spike the switch to ensure that the culture would continue forward and not fall back into old habits. To spike the switches, we put in place several changes in organizational and management processes to support the new direction.

7. *Learn from the journey.* We understood that this would not be the last time we undertook significant cultural change. This would be an ongoing effort to keep the company moving in the right direction. We took time to take stock of the learnings we experienced, so we could replicate the successes and avoid repeating the failures in the future.

PART

II

CLARIFYING THE VISION

The first step in creating culture change is to be clear on where we want to go—our vision for why we are making the change. We needed to ensure that everyone across the company understood the vision, the Five Guiding Principles, and *how* we planned to achieve our vision by creating a new culture for the company.

CHAPTER 3

CN's Five Guiding Principles

CN was already best-in-class. But we wanted more—we wanted to transform our industry—an opportunity very few people are granted during their lives. We wanted to achieve unheard-of levels of total shareholder return, customer service, asset utilization, and employee safety: We wanted it all.

To achieve such levels of success, we had to create ownership for Hunter Harrison's vision of the Five Guiding Principles. They created a path that employees could follow and a foundation for the culture we were trying to create. (See Figure 3.1.)

When Hunter first developed the Five Guiding Principles, he was reluctant to even write them down, because he did not want "corporate mission gibberish" posters on the walls for everyone to ignore. These principles had to be *real for everyone,* more than words on a page. Employees had to know them and apply them every day.

In 2003, to ensure employees knew and understood the principles, Hunter started sharing them throughout the company, and asking employees what the principles meant to them. As he met and worked with employees, the principles began to take shape.

Following are the simple definitions developed through that process that make the Five Guiding Principles come to life each day. (For more details and examples of the Five Guiding Principles, see E. Hunter Harrison, *How We Work and Why,* published by Canadian National Railway Company, 2005).

Figure 3.1   CN's Five Guiding Principles

Source: E. Hunter Harrison, *Change, Leadership, Mud and Why,* © 2008 Canadian National Railway Company.

Principle 1: Service—Doing What We Say We'll Do

- Do what you say you are going to do.
- "In the beginning was the customer." If you don't buy into that, you are missing the entire point.
- Listen better to everyone.
- Get faster. What can you do in your job to make CN a faster railway, without compromising Principle 4 (Safety)?
- Get more reliable. What can you do in your job to make CN a more reliable railway?
- Better service (speed and reliability) means our customers can carry smaller inventories and courier companies can rely on us to move their land-based packages.
- Faster transit times let us support the hourly rate for our unionized employees, giving them the best paychecks in the industry.

Principle 2: Cost Control—Achieved through Continually Fine-Tuning Processes

- It's *cost control,* not cost-cutting. There is a big difference.
- Continually refine the processes under your control. Doing it right the first time always costs less.

- If you truly need more money to make CN better—ask. If you have some left over, give it back—before we ask.
- Look at everything. A thousand little things add up to lots of money.

Principle 3: Asset Utilization—Maximized through Continually Fine-Tuning Processes

- This is the missing ingredient in the recipe for success in the rail industry.
- An asset is a liability until you put it to use. Assets must earn their keep. Don't sit on your assets.
- Look at every asset and ask: Do we really need it? Can someone else make better use of it? How can I get 24 hours out of it every day?
- Our estimates say we can probably do 10 to 15 percent more business using just what we have today. How can you make it happen?
- If you didn't use it last year, you probably won't this year. Scrap it, sell it, recycle it. Just get it out of the way.
- Better asset use means shorter cycle time for our equipment and customers, and we can move more with the same equipment. Each locomotive we don't need to buy saves $2 million, and each railcar saves $90,000 to $100,000. (If CN had offered today's service and reliability 20 years ago, one customer said he would have purchased 10,000 fewer railcars for his private fleet.)

Principle 4: Safety—Means 100 Percent Compliance 100 Percent of the Time

- Don't have injuries, don't have accidents.
- Look after each other's safety.
- Never overlook even the slightest rule infraction. You're not giving anyone a break—you're letting them risk injury to themselves and others.

Principle 5: People—CN is Powered by Passionate People

- Without people, the other principles have no meaning.
- Take people to their level of excellence.
- Nurture each other.

"The Five Guiding Principles are not rocket science," as Hunter notes. "They are simple concepts that have been tested by fire and survived in the real world."

People are the base on which CN builds everything. Without the right people doing the right things, CN can't deliver its product—Service. People always come first, but the other Guiding Principles are equally important.

These Five Guiding Principles are the pillars upon which Hunter built the cultural turnaround. Today, CN's employees think the Guiding Principles constantly—they are simple, and they work. Thinking this way set the stage for further culture change.

The Culture of
Precision Railroading

Understanding of and commitment to success in the Five Guiding Principles was spreading. Now was the time to assess the current culture and determine what future culture was needed to support continuous improvement.

Hunter studied how to achieve this culture change with two of his leaders (both part of this book's author team): Les Dakens, who was Senior Vice President, People at the time, and Peter Edwards, who was head of Organization Development. To build a true performance-oriented culture, they quickly settled on three foundational concepts that had underpinned success so far:

1. *The Organizational Culture Continuum*—a model that views organizations in five levels, from "out of control" to fully "engaged."
2. *The Spectrum of Employee Engagement*—a model showing how employees vary in their degree of engagement. They range from negative leaders and followers, through a large neutral majority, to positive leaders and followers.
3. *Washing out the mud in the middle*—"mud," a favorite term of Hunter's, refers to the bureaucracy, silos, poor communications, and disconnects that muddy the processes and workflow between top leaders and the front line.

Each of these concepts is important—not only to the CN story, but to any leader who is determined to change corporate culture.

The Organizational Culture Continuum

The first foundational concept was the *Organizational Culture Continuum*, a model developed by Peter Edwards. The model looks at cultures as operating along a continuum of five distinct levels, ranging from "out of control" to the ultimate goal of fully "engaged."

The goal of any organization is to get all employees on the engaged end of the continuum. It is here that employees contribute their maximum "Discretionary Performance^{SM}," which means performing their best because they *want* to, not because someone says they *have* to.

In the model (shown in Figure 4.1), note the descriptions under each category. Try taking a quick mental census of your own organization against the five levels. You will probably recognize each part of your organization as being at a specific level along the continuum.

Using the Organizational Culture Continuum to understand CN's culture, Hunter, Les, and Peter assessed each area of CN to

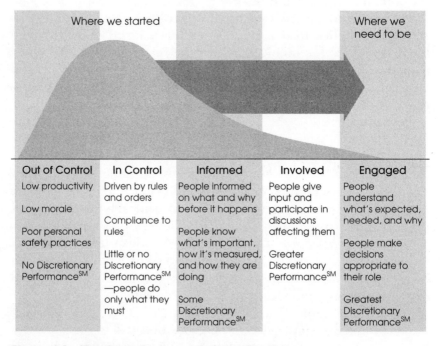

Out of Control	In Control	Informed	Involved	Engaged
Low productivity	Driven by rules and orders	People informed on what and why before it happens	People give input and participate in discussions affecting them	People understand what's expected, needed, and why
Low morale				
	Compliance to rules	People know what's important, how it's measured, and how they are doing	Greater Discretionary Performance^{SM}	People make decisions appropriate to their role
Poor personal safety practices				
	Little or no Discretionary Performance^{SM}			
No Discretionary Performance^{SM}	—people do only what they must			Greatest Discretionary Performance^{SM}
		Some Discretionary Performance^{SM}		

Figure 4.1   The Organizational Culture Continuum
Source: Adapted from materials provided by Peter Edwards.

measure where it stood on the continuum. What they discovered varied widely by location, function, and even across individuals. This was expected, given the different cultures that had been merged during the multiple acquisitions of other railways. Some areas had employees who were informed, involved, and even engaged.

But too many areas in CN showed left-column traits: low productivity, low morale, and poor personal safety. In addition, it appeared that employees lacked the motivation to perform and were doing only the minimum necessary to get by.

It was a humbling fact that while some parts of CN were in good shape, other parts were on the far left—out of control. Too many employees were doing as they wished, irrespective of business needs, safety rules, and company policies. CN had a long way to go to move these groups from out of control to fully engaged.

In an out of control organization, people have lots of freedom—they can do whatever they want—but there is little or no accountability for the results. Employees seek the easy way, the way that's most rewarding for them. In this situation, some leaders abuse the lack of standards and leadership through permissive practices. Worse, they multiply their damage by leading good people astray.

This is what CN had to change to survive. If the company failed to change, then its employees, customers, pensioners, and the many communities that are home to thousands of CN employees would be left in the lurch—all because some leaders didn't do the right thing by holding people accountable for results.

The Spectrum of Employee Engagement

The second foundational concept was based on the belief that the key to changing CN's culture is people. The concept we used again came from Peter Edwards—what he calls the *Spectrum of Employee Engagement* model.

In every organization, there is a range of employee engagement. Some employees are positively engaged, while others view the company in a negative way.

In every group of employees, there are those who are considered to be natural leaders. Some are positive leaders who support the company; some are negative leaders who regularly work against the company. Both positive and negative leaders often

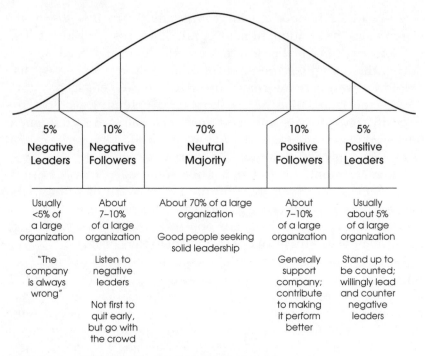

5%	10%	70%	10%	5%
Negative Leaders	Negative Followers	Neutral Majority	Positive Followers	Positive Leaders

Usually <5% of a large organization	About 7–10% of a large organization	About 70% of a large organization	About 7–10% of a large organization	Usually about 5% of a large organization
"The company is always wrong"	Listen to negative leaders	Good people seeking solid leadership	Generally support company; contribute to making it perform better	Stand up to be counted; willingly lead and counter negative leaders
	Not first to quit early, but go with the crowd			

Figure 4.2   The Spectrum of Employee Engagement
Source: Adapted from materials provided by Peter Edwards.

have followers who listen to their every word. Most importantly, there is a big 70 percent neutral majority who are simply looking for solid leadership. Overall, the distribution can appear as shown in Figure 4.2, although the real distribution varies widely among organizations.

The role of the neutral majority is critical. Given positive leadership, the right direction, and recognition, they become an incredible force that moves the organization miles ahead of competitors. However, organizations abhor a vacuum: if positive leaders are absent, negative leaders will fill the vacuum and (mis)lead the neutral majority, causing the culture to decay.

The Role of Organizational Leaders

The organization's leaders, from supervisor through executive, need the skills and fortitude to deal with each of these groups. The company must recognize, reward, and develop the positive leaders.

If that is done, more positive followers will become leaders, and the neutral majority will shift toward the positive end of this spectrum.

At the same time, the company needs to correct and reshape negative leaders. They must be stopped from getting away with breaking rules. They must stop being rewarded with attention for starting rumors. And they must be held accountable for their actions. If negative leaders refuse to change, they cannot stay.

By addressing the behaviors of negative leaders instead of ignoring them, CN began to demonstrate that being a negative leader is no longer desirable. And the neutrals who watch both ends of the spectrum to determine which looks more appealing will lean to the positive end. They will gravitate toward the positive leaders who can show them how to be valuable contributors to a viable business.

The catch was that CN's leadership team did not always understand this. At times, they unintentionally punished positive followers by giving them more work. They unintentionally rewarded negative followers by giving them the wrong kind of attention, such as listening to their whining.

When a negative leader is permitted to leave two hours early and earn the same pay as the positive leader who stays the full time, who is being rewarded? When a blatantly negative employee gets the same consideration for a special request as a positive employee, who is being rewarded?

It is up to the leaders of the organization to determine the culture they want to create. They exert great influence daily. The direction they give, the coaching they provide, the resources they provide or withhold, and the consequences they use to encourage or discourage certain behaviors—all these determine the culture and the performance of their group. When the spectrum weighs heavily negative, organizational leaders are failing in their job.

Washing Out the Mud in the Middle

The third foundational concept became known as "washing out the mud in the middle"—in reference to a favorite Hunter saying.

To understand this point, you need to understand the significance of mud to railroads. Mud—the kind you track into the kitchen—is a major destroyer of rail infrastructure.

Here is why: Deep beds of gravel are laid underneath railroad tracks. This gravel, called *railroad ballast*, creates a very stable, resilient bed to support the tracks. It also allows rainwater and snowmelt to drain quickly from the tracks.

The ballast gravel must be clean to let water drain. But inevitably, dust settles onto the gravel, it rains, and mud starts to accumulate—a little bit at first, and then it builds up rapidly. As the mud collects, it acts as an abrasive, grinding against the ballast gravel as heavy locomotives and railcars roll over it (for example, a fully loaded train hauling coal can weigh over 40 million pounds). And the mud is hidden within the gravel where you can't see it.

The result is expensive and potentially dangerous: Mud-filled ballast supports track less competently, which can allow rails to bend, leading to broken rails and derailments. Mud plugs up the ballast so it doesn't drain properly, retaining water that rots the wooden railroad ties—invisibly from underneath. Mud causes continual, expensive maintenance over CN's entire rail system of more than 20,000 miles.

Organizational Mud

Yet another form of mud is an invisible enemy throughout the railroad. As Hunter notes in his book, *Change, Leadership, Mud and Why,* "Over my career, I've found that organizations are much like track. If we're not careful, mud will creep in and stop the flow of clear communication between the leadership and where we really measure our success—the people who drive the spikes, move the cars, and deal with our customers."

This organizational mud is just as insidious as mud out on the tracks. Mud in the organization means bureaucracy, poor communications, silos, and disconnects between top leaders and the front line—anything that muddies processes as people try to work. The surprising thing about organizational mud is how many places it creeps in. (See Table 4.1.)

Mud is a bigger problem than most organizations realize, and they give too little attention to clearing it out. Mud suppresses good ideas, creates bad morale, wastes resources, and ultimately can ruin entire cultures and companies.

Mud in the Middle

Hunter talks about "mud in the middle." He is referring to the boggy confusion of conflicting direction and interpretations that can happen between the executive suite and frontline managers.

Table 4.1   Sources of Organizational Mud

Mud Source	Problems It Creates
Silos, poor communication, bureaucracy	An organization that creates silos automatically creates mud. If an organization becomes a bureaucracy, the mud just gets thicker.
Broken processes	Processes that are broken, out-of-date, out-of-step, or not followed—all create mud.
Fads	Flavor-of-the-month ideas that sound good but can't work create mud.
Too much data	Data is critical to success, but when data becomes so overwhelming that you don't know what's important, it creates mud.
Isolation behind our technology	Voice mail, e-mail, a BlackBerry®, text messages—all speed our business. But they are also tools that help us avoid talking face-to-face with a colleague. Anytime we try to resolve conflict without meeting face-to-face, mud can happen.

Executives are typically clear on their strategy and the direction they want to take, and first-line supervisors are clear about their day-to-day responsibilities of running the business. The problem is that communication between the two is never perfect. People hear different things from the same conversation. Written documents often fail to convey intent, and they can't check to see if the reader understands. Leaders have difficulty verifying that their intent is communicated. The problem gets multiplied by the other causes of mud.

Mud can appear at any level in the organization, but the greatest challenge lies with middle managers. They may distort or dilute the message. They may confuse the direction or issue with so many e-mails and approvals that first-line supervisors can't do their jobs. Management's job is to remove mud—remove the barriers to high performance. But that is sometimes lost in translating the executive's strategic goals.

The third foundation of CN's culture change was to wash out the mud in the middle. (See Figure 4.3.)

So these three foundational concepts, along with the strength in direction from the Five Guiding Principles, had set the stage for CN's culture change.

Figure 4.3   The Mud Pyramid
Source: Visualization of concept from E. Hunter Harrison, *Change, Leadership, Mud and Why,*
© 2008 Canadian National Railway.

This was not change for the sake of change. Hunter knew that his leadership team must be aligned and focused on changing the culture. CN needed to fundamentally change the culture to deliver continuous improvements quarter after quarter and remain the best in the industry.

PART
III

CHOOSING THE
RIGHT SWITCHPOINTS

With our vision clearly set and a solid understanding of our current culture, we had to determine how to change that culture into one of an engaged, committed workforce. We needed to identify which switchpoints would set us on the right route to faster culture change.

CHAPTER 5

How to Change CN's Culture?

For CN's new culture, a majority of the workforce needed to be at the "Engaged" end of the culture continuum. The question was how to get them there. *How could we change CN's culture? How could we achieve better leadership for engagement?*

Under Paul Tellier, CN had instituted a leadership development program for CN's top executives. It paired a high-quality assessment process conducted by Personnel Decisions International (PDI) with executive coaching of leaders by the Continuous Learning Group (CLG).

When Les Dakens worked for the H. J. Heinz Company, he saw the work done by CLG and the executive coaching delivered by CLG's Ned Morse. So he invited Ned to Montreal to discuss the coaching needs of several CN senior leaders.

Culture Equals Behavior

Ned met with Les and Peter Edwards, presenting CLG's executive coaching offering. But he also explained that CLG's primary focus was on behavior-based change of entire workplace cultures. He explained how CLG's coaching services had been developed to support their culture-change engagements.

The three talked about culture. The standard definitions of *culture* left them cold—vague statements like "culture is common values" or "culture is shared beliefs."

Ned shared CLG's definition of culture:

- "Culture is the patterns of behaviors . . .
- that are encouraged or discouraged . . .
- by people and systems . . .
- over time."

And then Ned employed a story to illustrate the definition:

Imagine you are new to a team, attending your first meeting. Your new boss says, "I like it when people speak up during these meetings!" She describes a problem the unit is facing, and asks the group for ideas.

You chime in. As you speak, you notice that your boss folds her arms, furrows her brow, breaks eye contact, and looks away from you. You also notice that your new teammates have broken eye contact with you, are leaning a bit away, and are scribbling in their notebooks.

When you are done talking, there is an awkward silence. Your boss clears her throat, neglects to thank you, and launches into her own solution to the problem. You observe your new colleagues leaning toward her, making eye contact, nodding, and taking notes.

A few minutes later, your boss asks if anyone has an idea how to solve another problem—a problem you actually worked on in your previous assignment.

What do you do? Speak up or keep quiet?

Most people would keep quiet, reacting to the earlier chilly reception. A cultural anthropologist would say that the new person had taken a step toward being *acculturated* and had learned a valuable lesson about the real culture of this workplace.

Ned then applied the science of behavior analysis to the situation. The science looks at environmental factors for why we behave the way we do. It is the basis for CLG's definition of culture:

- There was a pattern of behavior (speaking up) . . .
- That was encouraged or discouraged (in this case, discouraged) . . .

- By people and systems (in this case, the boss and peers) . . .
- Over time (in this case, three minutes).

He analyzed it further:

- There was a second pattern of behavior (the boss being "always right") . . .
- That was encouraged or discouraged (encouraged) . . .
- By people and systems (her colleagues) . . .
- Over time (in this case, developed over months and years).

Ned had made his point. The behavioral definition of culture made sense. Then he said, "Using this definition, we can frame everything that you and Hunter want to do, in very actionable steps:

- Identify the patterns of behavior (that you want and don't want) . . .
- To encourage and discourage . . .
- By people (the behavior of leaders) and systems (how you set up and manage your organizational systems) . . .
- Over time (long enough to make it stick)."

Ned made a final point: "The tough part is learning to be precise in identifying behaviors and getting good at effectively encouraging the behaviors you want and discouraging the ones you don't. This is where the science of behavior helps."

Les and Peter were encouraged. Ned's behavioral science solution matched their beliefs about how they needed to change the culture, and provided a clear path for action.

CHAPTER 6

Creating a Culture of Discretionary Performance℠

The plan was to use CLG's application of the science of behavior to encourage CN's positive leaders and discourage the negative leaders, moving the culture from "Out of Control" toward "Engaged," thereby capturing employees' Discretionary Performance℠ to achieve unprecedented levels of performance.

The Discretionary Performance℠ Model shows the difference in performance in organizations where people *have to* perform to avoid negative consequences versus *want to* perform because they are motivated by positive consequences. This is why CN's leaders needed to engage employees. By engaging them, leaders developed a far greater percentage of employees who would give CN their Discretionary Performance℠.

Leaders who talk to employees only when something is wrong create a punishing workplace, guaranteed to discourage employees' best performance. In this environment, employees will adhere to the rules and comply with leaders' demands, but nothing more. They will deliver only the results they have to. They won't stick out their necks to go above and beyond. Why should they? If employees step outside the box and try a better way, they will either get stomped or no one will notice. It's safer to comply and stay quiet.

But when effective leaders create the right conditions, they inspire and engage employees to go way beyond the expected.

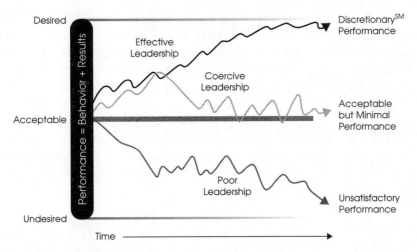

Figure 6.1   The Discretionary Performance℠ Model
Source: Discretionary Performance℠ is a service mark of CLG.

Effective leaders inspire employees to deliver their best through creating a balanced environment. They:

- Maintain exceptionally high standards.
- Encourage and recognize employees' extra effort.
- Inspire want-to performance.

Employees not only do their jobs, but devise ways to do them smarter, better, faster, cheaper. When employees go above and beyond like this, they are demonstrating Discretionary Performance℠— the difference in the energy, enthusiasm, and commitment when doing something because you *want* to, instead of because you *have* to. (See Figure 6.1.)

We all want to believe that what we do daily really *matters* and *makes a difference*. We want something we can feel good about and commit to. When we do, it is very powerful for everyone.

What's in It for the Employee?

Cynics might say this is good for the company, but there's nothing in it for the employee. Nothing could be further from the truth! Effective leaders encourage people to develop their potential and contribute in meaningful ways.

Typically, their jobs become broader, more interesting, and they have a greater measure of control. They are winning and feel like they are. So when the inevitable changes occur, they can be the ones driving the change, rather than being driven by it.

We all spend a big piece of our lives at work, so it is very important to us. The worst message a leader can send is that an employee doesn't really matter—even if that message is unintentional.

Effective leaders are essential in creating an organization where employees are expected to, are able to, and want to contribute their best, and know that they are. In this environment, people grow.

CHAPTER

Creating Q4 Leaders
to Drive Change

Exactly *what characteristics would CN's desired leaders display?* Managers and supervisors needed to understand the desired new leadership style.

The problem was that it couldn't be captured easily. It was more of a feeling, a set of values, an understanding of how to work with employees, and an internal drive to be the best leader possible. We just knew it when we saw it.

Culture Change Begins with Leadership

Since culture equals behavior, we needed to define the culture by defining the behaviors that would deliver results. To change culture means to change behavior. This starts at the top, with the organization's leadership.

The first behavior that leaders need to develop is to connect better with their people. It all goes back to leaders focusing on achieving superior business results *the right way:* by driving accountability through respect, engagement, and commitment to employees. Leaders who balance a hard focus on results with commitment to their employees are the ones who can drive and sustain high-performing organizations.

Such leaders get results through two types of behaviors:

1. *Results-driven behaviors (the "what").* This is the hard side of leadership. Results-driven behaviors are directly related to getting the job done. (Example: Always be crystal clear on the target results; review team progress weekly.)
2. *Engagement-focused behaviors (the "how").* This is the soft side of leadership. Engagement-focused behaviors are how leaders go about engaging others. (Example: Don't keep problems to yourself—engage with your team and seek their advice in problem solving.)

Both types of behaviors are critical to success. Effective leaders balance the two by being results-driven *and* engagement-focused (recognizing employees' skills and contributions). Leaders who master this balance create amazingly productive working environments, just like the one we were shaping. Such environments consistently produce strong results with high employee engagement and satisfaction.

The Q4 Leadership℠ Model

To understand how effective any leader is, look at two things: the leader's ability to deliver results *and* his effectiveness at engaging employees. A proven tool for this analysis is the Q4 Leadership℠ Model. Leaders viewed in light of this model fall into one of four quadrants. Understanding each quadrant helps leaders see where they are and what to change to become more effective. (See Figure 7.1.)

Leaders in each quadrant have very recognizable characteristics. As you read them here you'll instantly recognize leaders you know—including yourself.

Q1 Leader: Has ineffective leadership behaviors, creating inconsistent or poor business results. This leader doesn't set clear, consistent direction. He also has problems giving performance feedback—offers too little, or it's ineffective, or mostly negative, or gives none at all. The result is unhappy, completely disengaged employees and poor results, leading ultimately to business failure. Q1 leaders usually don't last very long. They are fired, demoted, or quit.

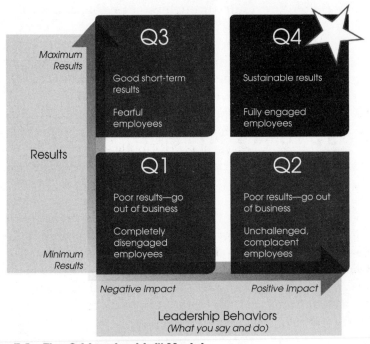

Figure 7.1   The Q4 Leadership℠ Model
Source: Q4 Leadership℠ Model is a service mark of CLG.

Q2 Leader: Appears to have effective leadership behaviors, but fails to give high priority to business results, so targets are often missed. This leader has difficulty requiring full compliance and evades issues to avoid upsetting employees. Employees may like working for this person, because they work hard to keep employees happy, often at the expense of getting results. But employees are unchallenged and complacent.

Q3 Leader: Has ineffective leadership behaviors, but gets short-term business results. This leader demands results based on his authority, using past events more to punish poor performance than for learning and development. Q3 leaders are often strong individual contributors, demanding compliance to practices they know work, but they don't know how to maximize their team's performance. Employees are fearfull, and thus are only as productive as they have to be.

Q4 Leader: Has effective leadership behaviors, and gets sustainable business results. This leader gives plenty of feedback, both positive and constructive, brings out people's best, and encourages them to be creative and deliver on goals. Employees are happy and committed, turnover is minimal, and the business thrives. This leader has found the sweet spot and will become noted and admired for doing the right things in the right way.

How Did CN Create Q4 Leaders?

Q4 leaders rarely just happen. Q4 Leadership℠ requires learning and practice.

Recalling the Spectrum of Employee Engagement in Chapter 4, leaders who take a balanced approach to their organization will develop a culture where positive leaders are recognized and negative leaders have little reason to stay negative. As CN began its culture change, we quickly discovered that management could not boast Q4 leaders across the board. Two unhealthy majorities had developed over time:

1. *Q3 leaders dominated the top of the house.* They were tough, good at getting short-term results, and knowledgeable about the business. But their style was to demand compliance, so they created unhappy employees who did the necessary minimum required, and no more.

   The organization relied on these Q3 leaders and their punishing style to achieve success. Indeed, they brought the culture under control and delivered the results needed to grow as a private company. But they did so through fear and intimidation, and that was not how CN's new culture was to be led.

2. *Q2 leaders permeated the first-line supervisor ranks.* They gave in to employee requests simply to make them happy and keep the peace. Consequently, they could not deliver results. These leaders were promoted from the ranks, given little training in how to supervise, and often sent to manage their employee friends.

   When they needed to hold people accountable, the only role models these Q2 leaders had were the hardball Q3 leaders above them. They knew what it felt like to be on the receiving end of Q3 leadership, and they didn't want to lead that way.

With little training in effective leadership, they resorted to being *friends* to the employees, shielding them from Q3 leaders. As Q2 frontline supervisors grew more protective, Q3 leaders grew louder. The Q2 leaders were caught in the middle.

No one had planned this cultural norm that thrived in various pockets of CN. The company had drifted into it, as many companies do. It had to change.

The challenge was to shift those areas of the organization from getting results through fear and intimidation (Q3) to getting results through *engaging* our employees (Q4). Engaging employees works much better: Employees admire leaders who recognize and reward behaviors that get results, while calling out unwanted behaviors and helping them to improve.

Once leaders came to terms with how they got results (or didn't) through their leadership, they set out to change things. To do this, they:

- Focused on employee behaviors that were critical to get results.
- Tracked the results and behaviors for the team to see.
- Provided objective, constructive feedback to employees who were not engaging in those behaviors.
- Provided positive feedback for those employees who were practicing those behaviors.
- Worked hard to do this consistently every day.

Leadership is like any other relationship in our lives: we get out of it what we put into it. When we spend time developing our people, our reward is employees who are engaged and committed, who share great ideas, and who help to continuously improve the business.

Changing Your Style Isn't Easy

Understanding the concept of how to lead the right way was the easy part. *Putting it into action was tough.* When people have a history of getting results using their current style (Q2 or Q3), and it works in its own way, why change?

Bruce Bierman is a CN leader—experienced, smart, and friendly. Bruce stands his ground like a post set in concrete. Bruce describes his difficult journey from Q3 leader to Q4:

> I was waiting for a call about my next promotion. But when the call came, it wasn't what I expected. It was a warning.
>
> For years, I had been a great Q3 leader, a get-it-done guy. However, I screamed and hollered my way to results.
>
> The call came from Senior Vice President Gordon Trafton. "Bruce, you better change how you deal with people, or you can't continue to work for this railroad. I will not tolerate yelling and screaming at managers and employees. You can either get on the bus with us, or leave us."
>
> That prompted some real soul searching. I'd done everything right, holding people accountable and getting results. What was I doing wrong?
>
> I called my supervisor. He said, "Bruce, you need to change your behaviors, or you'll be looking for another job." He gave me three hours of feedback, with examples of how my actions didn't fit CN's new culture. I felt dejected, but knew I must change.
>
> As a Q3 leader, I got results, but my leadership behavior was poor. Everyone either cooperated or felt my wrath. I didn't realize the effect of my tirades: I was building resentment, not a team. My reports did only the minimum needed to avoid my flames.
>
> Over the next year, I worked hard to put Q3 behaviors behind me. I listened more, got people together, and supported their ideas. It's hard to admit you must change, but it helps when your job is on the line.
>
> Jack Hinzman of CLG coached me with feedback on creating the right atmosphere for my managers to blossom. I learned that changing from Q3 to Q4 behaviors meant more than just no-more-yelling. I learned DCOM®:
>
> - How to give people *direction* without wrath.
> - How to coach my team to build their *competence.*
> - How to ensure they had the *opportunity* and resources to be successful.
> - How to *motivate* by giving positive feedback and holding people accountable without yelling.

I worked hard, was promoted, and brought together a team of railroaders who sharply improved Chicago operations.

But a survey showed I wasn't fully a Q4 Leader. The difference in my self-ratings and my team's said I had to keep working hard on my leadership style.

Recent feedback says I have finally transitioned from Q3 to Q4. My journey's greatest lesson: I have to work on my leadership skills every day, because being a Q4 leader requires continuous improvement. Looking back, I realize that it was either get on that bus, or get run over!

Building Leadership Fluency

As Bruce's story shows, moving to a new model of leadership requires tremendous trust that the new way of leading is better than the old way. It also requires patience. Just like learning any other skill, there is a definite learning progression. The Fluency Model℠ in Figure 7.2 shows the typical stages we all go through as we learn new things.

In the first stage, ignorance is bliss—we don't know what we don't know. Then we progress through stages where we become

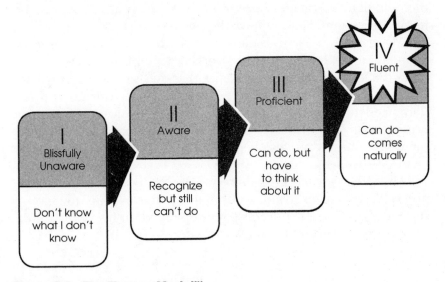

Figure 7.2 The Fluency Model℠
Source: The Fluency Model℠ is a service mark of CLG.

aware, then *proficient*, and finally arrive where we want to be: *fluent* in the new leadership style, where the new way of working simply becomes automatic.

If we apply the fluency model to learning to play golf, the four stages might look like this:

   I. Blissfully unaware: You decide to learn golf. You know nothing of the game, except that you need clubs, a ball, a golf course, and decent weather.

  II. Aware: Through training and watching a pro, you learn that you must face the right direction, hips aligned, and club face straight. Now you know what you need to do, but you have no proficiency. Your golfing partners nickname you "Duffer."

 III. Proficient: After practicing, you get so you can play when you concentrate, but if your mind wanders, you're toast. Your golfing partners nickname you "Bogey."

 IV. Fluent: You don't have to think about lining up your body or keeping your head down; you simply set up the ball and drive nearly automatically. Your golfing partners nickname you "Tiger."

Using these four steps as milestones, CN's leaders developed their ability to engage employees and get results. This model helped them understand where they were in the journey.

Along the way, some leaders became discouraged or felt worse about their leadership as they worked to improve it. When you know the Fluency Model, you realize that they were actually making progress, understanding there was another way to lead, and that they needed practice to master it (awareness stage). This model presented an opportunity to help those leaders not only understand the new way but also begin using the tools and techniques to be more effective.

All leaders started at their own place, progressed through this process at their own speed, and required their own unique level of support. Each leader's success truly depended on his ability to own the change and utilize the tools.

PART IV

SELECTING THE TOOLS FOR CHANGE

On the railroad, the right tools make the difference in an employee's ability to complete a job safely and efficiently. In culture change, having the right tools has a similar impact—you need the right tools to ensure change. We found the right tools in Behavioral Science.

The Science of the ABCs

To appreciate the dynamics of the culture change that CN was undertaking, it is important to understand the tools that are applied in the ongoing transformation. At the core of these tools is behavioral science, or what CN calls *the ABCs*.

The ABCs seek to explain the influences that cause people to take some actions and not others. The ABCs answer questions like:

- Why did he *do* that?
- Why did she *say* that?
- What caused the group's *actions*?

An understanding of what drives people's behavior is absolutely critical for creating conditions for a successful organization.

It's All about Behavior

A good analogy is how we obey traffic laws (or don't obey them). Many of us have exceeded the speed limit on occasion. It wasn't because we didn't know better. We had been trained on the traffic laws, saw the speed limit signs, and knew the potential of speed to cause an accident. But it looked clear, safe, and we thought we'd get away with it, so we broke the law against speeding. Yet whenever we encounter a red traffic light, we almost certainly stop.

Why do we obey some laws and not others? The answer is *consequences*, and understanding how to use consequences to manage human behavior is the core of behavioral science—the science behind CN's cultural revolution.

The ABCs of Behavior

Two decades ago, behavioral science was a fledgling in the business world, often regarded as consultant mumbo-jumbo. Some thought it too simple to be effective. Others feared that it was manipulative. But time, experience, and consistent results have refined the tools of the science. Today, it is a proven method for improving performance of organizations for the benefit of all.

The beauty of behavioral science is that it applies to any business or industry, at all levels from executive suite to front line. CN worked with CLG to adapt the science in the best manner for the railroad.

At CN, the application of behavioral science was called *the ABCs*. Today you hear people refer to the ABCs in CN's rail yards and corporate offices. The term *ABCs* comes from the ABC model on which behavioral science is built.

The ABC model shows the relationship of *antecedents, behaviors,* and *consequences*—hence the name, ABCs. The model shows that antecedents trigger your behavior, and the resulting consequences that you experience influence whether you repeat that behavior. This applies to every single behavior, every day. (See Figure 8.1.)

The CLG consulting team conducted training on the ABCs across the organization. One of this book's authors, Judy Johnson, was one of the coaches.

Figure 8.1   The ABC Model
Source: CLG.

When training the ABCs, Judy often used this classic example: You are hungry, which is the *antecedent* that triggers your *behavior* of trying a new restaurant. If the *consequence* that you experience is a great meal, you'll repeat the behavior of going to that restaurant. (And if the *consequence* is a lousy meal, you won't repeat the behavior.)

The ABCs Make Fundamental Sense

The ABC model resonated with CN's leaders because it made sense in their personal lives. Then, when we transitioned to work examples, everyone made the connection and understood how it worked.

Following are the essential things to know about A, B, and C.

A: Antecedents

Antecedents come before a behavior and trigger it. Sample antecedents include hunger, a ringing phone, a traffic light changing color, your alarm clock sounding off, or hearing someone say, "It's time for the meeting." These antecedents either set the stage for your behavior or trigger it to happen.

When the phone rings, you answer—or at least look to see who's calling. If a traffic light turns red, you stop. Hearing "It's time for the meeting" gets you moving to attend it. All are antecedents that trigger your behavior.

B: Behavior

Behavior is action—it is anything you say or do. Sample behaviors include attending a meeting, sending an e-mail, praising an employee, grabbing a coffee, and giving someone constructive feedback on a safety violation.

In culture change, some behaviors are more important than others. Behavioral science shows you how to pinpoint the specific, *measurable* behaviors that are key to successful culture change.

This may sound easy, but it requires a lot of skill. For example, CN managers tried to identify "behaviors that are critical for a leadership team." They thought they identified a good one: "committed to safety." Well, that sounds good, but it is not a behavior you can measure! How can you tell whether someone is "committed?" Actions speak louder than words, and in behavioral science, actions (behaviors) are everything.

To use the ABCs, ask what the leader actually *says or does* that demonstrates commitment to safety. For example, if the leader *tells his team* (a behavior), "I see tripping hazards in the warehouse—let's clean 'em up today!" and next morning he *visits* the warehouse (another behavior) to verify that all tripping hazards are gone, *that's behavior*—that is what he *said and did* to show he is committed to safety.

This is what we mean by *pinpointing* behaviors. If you intend to use consequences to manage people's behavior, you first must pinpoint the true behavior with great precision.

C: Consequences

Consequences follow the behavior. They influence whether you will repeat it or not. Consequences are all around us and drive every behavior.

Some behaviors have *positive* consequences:

- *Antecedent:* Your phone rings. Caller ID shows it is your helpful co-worker Bill.
- *Behavior:* You answer the phone.
- *Consequence:* Bill gives you valuable feedback that you need for your next meeting, so you are likely to answer his calls in the future. (This positive consequence drives your future behavior of answering when he calls.)

Behaviors can have *negative* consequences, too. These reduce the likelihood of your repeating the behavior:

- *Antecedent:* Your phone rings. Caller ID shows it's your peer Sara, with whom you have an edgy relationship.
- *Behavior:* You answer the phone, wincing a little.
- *Consequence:* Sara demands details on your work last week because she doesn't trust your sales report. She ties you up for an hour discussing what should have been resolved in five minutes. You just lost 55 minutes in which you could have been selling. Next time she calls, you'll let it roll into voice mail. (This negative consequence drives your future behavior of avoiding her calls.)

The ABCs apply to every single thing you and your employees do, no exceptions (think about it). That's why behavioral science works.

If it sounds simple, it is—but that's deceptive. Actually applying the ABCs takes practice, coaching, and consistent use to get the full value. That is why CN chose to partner with CLG. Their consultants' depth in applying behavioral science to improve organizations and cultures and their 24/7 approach to coaching were exactly what CN needed.

The Commanding Power of Consequences

Consequences are the key to changing behavior, which is the key to changing a culture. While both antecedents and consequences are necessary for behaviors to happen, consequences are much more powerful. Consequences have four times more influence on behaviors than antecedents do. (See Figure 9.1.)

If you understand consequences, you can work wonders to improve the performance and quality of life in your organization.

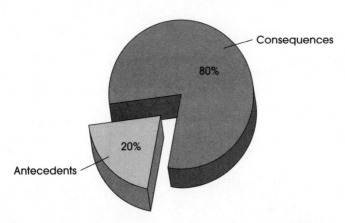

Figure 9.1   Consequences Have a Much Greater Influence on Behavior than Antecedents
Source: CLG.

Consequences vary widely in their power, depending on four major factors. The impact of a consequence on any behavior depends on four components that are described in CLG's E-TIP Analysis℠ model (for more information on this model, see Leslie Braksick, *Unlock Behavior, Unleash Profits,* second edition, published by McGraw-Hill in 2007):

1. *Timing* (immediately after the behavior, or delayed?).
2. *Importance* to the recipient (high or low?).
3. *Probability* of recurring (high or low?).
4. *Where it comes from* (there are five sources, as you will see).

The campaign to stop early quits drew upon all of these factors to ensure the right consequences supported the behavior change.

Timing

If you do something well and someone immediately acknowledges your efforts, that's far more powerful than getting a thank-you letter three months later. If you arrive early at work and therefore have first pick of the tasks you do that day, that is an immediate positive consequence for arriving early. *Immediate consequences are always stronger than delayed ones.*

When leaders know that the timing of a consequence is important, they take certain measures to provide immediate feedback. Taking the time to walk a direct report out of an important meeting in order to give the person feedback about his or her presentation is an example of an immediate consequence. Another immediate consequence would be correcting a co-worker who is acting unsafely, right when you see it.

The lesson for Q4 leaders: Especially during culture change, apply consequences immediately for greatest impact.

Importance to Recipient

If you do something and your boss says, "Wow! Terrific job! You made my day!" that feedback is of high importance to you. If the feedback comes from an administrative clerk on the third floor whom you barely know, it may be less important to you. *The more important the consequence is to you, the stronger it is.*

Importance of the consequence is why we worked with each supervisor to identify what kind of personal recognition would have the greatest value for each team member. People vary widely in how they like to be recognized. Some enjoy a public show of thanks, like a handshake in front of their co-workers. Others prefer a quiet, private show of appreciation, such as an e-mail or a quick note.

The lesson for Q4 leaders: Especially during culture change, make sure the consequence is truly important to the individual for greatest impact.

Probability of Recurring

If your boss lets you know every time you do a really good job, then you know that there is a high probability of being commended when you do well. But if the thanks is hit-or-miss, the probability of your receiving it is low. *High-probability consequences are always stronger than low-probability ones.*

Employees who consistently receive feedback from their managers would say that there is a high probability that they will receive feedback for an upcoming presentation. On the contrary, employees who see their managers sporadically, and talk with them only about the current problem of the day, would report the probability of receiving feedback as low.

The lesson for Q4 leaders: Especially during culture change, deliver consequences often and consistently until you see that performance results are being met. Then keep delivering consequences as needed to sustain the change.

Where Does the Consequence Come From?

Understanding the power of consequences—based on their timing, importance to the individual, and probability of recurring—helps you understand why someone behaves the way they do. Another important aspect of a consequence is where it comes from.

There are five basic sources of consequences: nature, yourself, your peers, management, and the organization. They have a definite hierarchy of impact, as shown in Figure 9.2.

The strongest consequences are at the bottom of the pyramid: *natural consequences.* The quiet you enjoy by closing your office door, the pleasurable chitchat with co-workers in the hallway, and

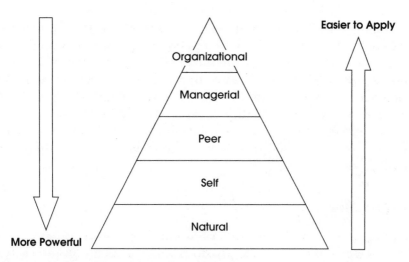

Figure 9.2 The Consequence Pyramid℠

Source: The Consequence Pyramid℠ is a service mark of CLG.

the pain of blisters from wearing ill-fitting shoes are all naturally occurring consequences.

Next in strength are *self-consequences*—those that we give ourselves. Examples include self-talk such as "I can see that I'm making a difference," "I did a good job and I know it," or "I should have been better prepared for the meeting."

Moving up the pyramid, getting less strong, are *peer consequences.* Examples are a co-worker's glare at you from across the conference table, a pat on the back, razzing in the lunchroom, or smiling co-workers who welcome you back from a trip.

Weaker yet are *managerial consequences.* These are consequences that you directly provide as a manager or supervisor. They include feedback, performance reviews, and job assignments. Although your personal feedback to someone can have an impact, like it or not, peer pressure is often stronger. This is why culture change requires engaging employees in the change (pushing the consequences lower on the pyramid) instead of demanding compliance.

Finally, at the top of the pyramid are the least powerful, *organizational consequences.* These include annual pay increases, bonus pay, demerits, attendance awards, or President's Circle membership. How can we say organizational consequences are least powerful? Organizational consequences are often delayed and poorly linked to employee performance, so they are unlikely to drive performance in the future.

Does this mean that managerial and organizational consequences are useless? No, it's just that they are less powerful overall than peer, self-, and natural consequences.

The relative weakness of organizational consequences explains why attendance award programs don't work very well. All it takes is a little peer pressure from a few employees who say, "Coming to work on time is sucking up!" Thus, a well-intentioned *positive organizational consequence* becomes instantly out-shouted by a stronger *negative peer consequence.*

Another reason that attendance rewards are weak in effect is that soon you hear employees saying, "I'll be late tomorrow, so I won't get the attendance award. But that's okay, because I hate getting up on stage—it means a week of harassment from my co-workers!" (Thus a well-intended positive consequence turns into a negative consequence.)

Despite the fact that managerial consequences have less power, they can still be a critical change tool. The key is to understand the relationship between the sources of consequences and their relative power.

The lesson for Q4 leaders: Especially during culture change, try to use consequences that are lower on the consequence pyramid.

Which Consequences Should I Use?

Clearly, if you really want to help employees change, you cannot rely solely on relatively weak organizational consequences. So what do you do? Two things:

1. Be close to your employees so you fully understand the most powerful influences on them—peer, self-, and natural consequences.
2. Provide consequences that will best support the behavior you need—consequences that are positive, immediate, highly important to individuals, high-probability, and coming from a variety of sources.

In creating culture change, we often have to start with consequences that are easy to deliver—organizational and managerial consequences. These can get new behavior started and are consistent across the organization. However, the change typically won't last unless other, more powerful consequences are there to support it.

That's where peer, self-, and even naturally occurring consequences come into play. When employees are engaged in a culture change, you see peer and self-consequences emerge. And when leaders seek to change work processes to support the new culture, natural consequences follow.

It is only when you have the consequences coming primarily from the bottom of the pyramid—with the organization and management consequences backing them up, but not being the primary consequence sources—that you truly change the culture.

Consequences and Culture Change

So the hard reality of culture change is this: *The easiest consequences to administer (managerial and organizational) are the least effective at changing behavior. And the hardest to administer (natural, self-, peer) are the most powerful.* At CN, we relearned this lesson over and over. Corporate mandates have little influence compared to an employee's peers (meaning the union and co-workers), which push them the other way.

As we go through our daily lives, we behave constantly, generating a big array of consequences for ourselves and others. That combination of consequences influences which behaviors we repeat and which we don't.

At CN, as leaders and agents of culture change, the more we understood how antecedents and consequences influenced behavior in our organization, the better we were able to help employees navigate the change process.

Authors' Note: Doing the Right Thing with the ABCs

The science of behavior never sleeps. It explains what we do. What you predict as the likely consequences from your behavior, combined with what you find positive or negative, determines how you behave.

Learning how to align consequences more effectively to get the behaviors you need at work puts a very powerful tool into your hands. It can significantly impact people's lives.

Along with the knowledge of how to harness this science comes an ethical obligation to use it for the benefit of everyone. This means always using our knowledge of what drives behavior to make the work environment better, more productive, and fulfilling.

Fundamentally, the ABCs and Q4 Leadership^{SM} teach leaders about the influence that the *work environment* has on people's choices. It is the work environment (which includes all the people around us), with all its antecedents and consequences, that influences employees' behavior. Our work environment constantly influences our choices of what to do or not do.

As leaders, we create the work environment—we provide many antecedents and consequences. So it is our responsibility to use the ABCs to create an atmosphere that positively influences the choices that employees make.

Everyone influences people around them every day by providing antecedents and consequences. Sometimes we do so purposefully with knowledge and skill. Sometimes we do it unknowingly. Either way, we still influence the behavior of others. (Think about your typical day, and you will see that this is true, both at work and at home.)

We at CN and CLG choose to use the ABCs and Q4 Leadership^{SM} to help people improve behaviors that are important to them and to the business—behaviors like working safely so they get home healthy and sound. And behaviors that help us run a safe, profitable, successful railroad so they have a future with CN.

CHAPTER

10

The ABC Toolkit

To truly effect change, we pulled the basic ABCs into a useful model that showed leaders how to link behavior to the results they needed to achieve. We called it the *ABC Toolkit*.

The Five-Step Model

The core of the ABC Toolkit is a five-step model:

1. *Identify* your target results to be achieved.
2. *Pinpoint* the performers and their critical behaviors.
3. *Analyze* the behaviors.
4. *Measure* the behaviors and results.
5. *Coach* to increase the desired behaviors.

This model guided leaders through a proven problem-solving approach. By following its steps, they learned how to select the right behaviors to support the Five Guiding Principles. They also learned how to coach employees in doing those behaviors.

The beauty of the ABC Toolkit is that it is easy to follow. Once you get it, it seems like common sense—so logical that you wonder why it's not used everywhere. Figure 10.1 shows the five-step toolkit. What follows is a brief explanation of how each step works.

Step 1: Identify Targeted Results

Leaders require a reason for leading—in other words, a vision. In our case, the vision is the Five Guiding Principles (Service, Cost

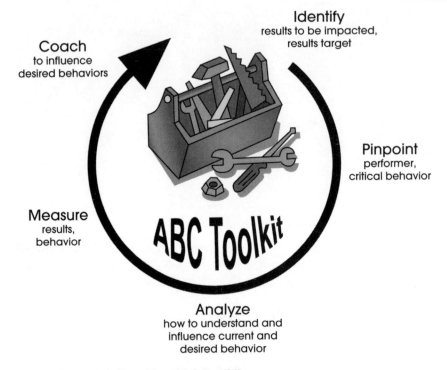

Identify
results to be impacted,
results target

Coach
to influence
desired behaviors

Pinpoint
performer,
critical behavior

Measure
results,
behavior

ABC Toolkit

Analyze
how to understand and
influence current and
desired behavior

Figure 10.1   The Five-Step ABC Toolkit
Source: © 2004 Canadian National Railway Company and CLG.

Control, Asset Utilization, Safety, and People). To translate those principles into real behaviors, leaders start by deciding which of the principles is most critical in their organization.

Then they ask, *what target result can my team influence today that will impact this Guiding Principle?* The more clearly employees see the link between their daily behavior and the profitability of the company, the more likely they will be to work toward improving that profit:

My daily behavior = CN's results

As an example to help illustrate these steps, imagine that a mechanic who repairs locomotives can't see how his daily work impacts CN's operating ratio at year's end. All he sees is the impact that his work has inside the shop. He sees how improving the maintenance process can reduce the time spent, which reduces cost and lets him move on to work on another locomotive. But that's all he sees. He doesn't see the larger picture, in which every employee's work is linked to CN's operating ratio.

We choose the target result in such a way that employees can honestly answer *yes* to all of these questions:

- Am I accountable for these results?
- Can I impact them?
- Are these results achievable in 30 to 90 days?
- Is this a priority for me and my team?
- Does this result contribute to at least one of CN's Five Guiding Principles? Which ones?

By using these questions to get clear on a near-term result, employees can then see the alignment between what they do today and the company's profits by the end of the year.

This backward chaining of results helps both leaders and employees see how they can influence something as broad as our guiding principle of Service.

Step 2: Pinpoint Performers and Behaviors

Once the target result is clear, the next step is to identify *who* has to do *what* to achieve it (in other words, the behavior). First, we identify employees who have the greatest impact on the target result. Then we pinpoint which of their behaviors are most critical to achieving the result.

By pinpointing the employees and behaviors most critical for attaining the desired result, we draw an even tighter line between employees and results. It also helps make crystal clear to each employee what we expect of him.

In our example of the mechanic, we select behaviors that contribute to obtaining the operating ratio. Those behaviors might be the way he prioritizes work for the day, or using a new three-step process to do maintenance, or even his behavior of taking time to fix it right the first time so the same locomotive will not be out of service again next week.

Step 3: Analyze, Using the ABCs and DCOM®

Then it is time to use the ABCs to analyze the pinpointed behaviors. We must identify the antecedents and consequences that drive the behaviors. Once we have a clear grasp of the consequences, we can use them to strengthen the critical behaviors.

CLG created a research-based, easy-to-remember tool called the DCOM® Model to assess the antecedents and consequences for each behavior. We use the DCOM® Model to analyze the four building blocks of high-performance people and companies:

1. *Direction* is a clear statement of the work priorities and desired behaviors on the part of employees. Direction aligns what employees do with the desired result. Direction gives the context for employee performance.
2. *Competence* is the individual's (and organization's) ability to perform, including technical, management, business, and interpersonal skills.
3. *Opportunity* is the availability of all needed resources, such as technology, processes, training, tools, time, funding, and authority.
4. *Motivation* is the driver of performance, resulting from the consequences of employees' behaviors.

The ABC analysis and DCOM® are closely related, as shown in Figure 10.2.

On the left in the model, Direction, Competence, and Opportunity are all antecedents. This means that they set the stage

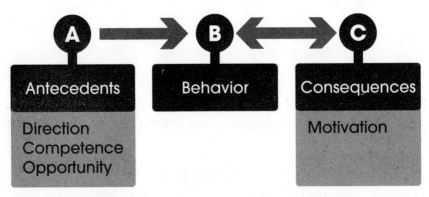

Figure 10.2 Relationship of the ABC Analysis and DCOM®
Source: DCOM® is a registered trademark of CLG.

for successful behavior and trigger it. They are essential for effective leadership and are the basis for a fluid and resilient organization. On the right, consequences provide the Motivation that is the key to high performance.

Effective leaders consistently pair D, C, and O antecedents with M (motivating) consequences to get the desired behaviors. This enables everyone to perform to his full potential.

For our mechanic who is working to fix his locomotives right the first time, an ABC analysis reveals antecedents that promote the wrong behaviors:

- Nagging, disruptive phone calls: "How fast can you get that done?!"
- Lack of training in how to analyze the root cause of symptoms.

The ABC analysis also reveals consequences that promote the wrong behaviors:

- Reviewing results in weekly meetings that focus solely on the speed of fixing locomotives (this sends the message that speed takes priority over quality and completeness).
- Criticism from the boss for taking too long, because the mechanic tried to do his best work.

Those are the wrong antecedents and consequences, so obviously we must change them for the mechanic to do his best work. (Maybe then he will even *enjoy* his work, thus generating Discretionary Performance℠.) Once you see the diagram, it seems pretty obvious. But the power of DCOM® lies in the discipline it creates in leaders' thinking.

CLG consultant Steve Quesnelle worked extensively in CN's Western Region. He tells this story of how using DCOM® helped one group achieve a quick breakthrough to fix a nagging problem:

> I was working with CN's Bridges and Structures team on a thorny issue that plagued their leader. Steve Del Vecchio, a senior manager, was frustrated by his team's inconsistent submission of weekly field reports. These reports had recently been

changed to an e-mail format to make them easier and faster to submit.

Every Monday, when Steve met with his boss to go over the reports, he was missing some of them, and thus had an incomplete picture of the past week's activities.

As Steve's ABC coach, I asked if I could help facilitate a meeting to ensure that the field would e-mail complete and timely weekly reports.

We met with his managers and asked what was getting in the way of submitting the weekly reports. Admirably, the team took responsibility, saying they had not provided enough Direction (the "D" in DCOM®) on this issue. So we worked on a communication plan to reinforce to all field supervisors the importance of e-mailing their reports every Friday, and they all committed to the plan.

Then I did the good consultant thing, and asked a dumb question: "Okay, guys, who is willing to bet their next paycheck that Steve Del Vecchio will have your report every Monday as planned?"

All hands shot up—except one. Bingo! Now we were getting somewhere.

I looked at the gentleman and asked, "Why not?"

"Well," he said, "a couple of my guys don't have computers."

Steve Del Vecchio quickly agreed to sign a purchase order for two new laptops.

I asked again: "Okay, *now* who is willing to bet their next paycheck that Steve will have his report every Monday?"

As expected, all hands now shot up.

Then I asked dumb question number two: "Those two supervisors who don't have computers . . . when they get their laptops, do they by any chance know how to use them?"

"Gee, I guess not," the manager replied.

If we had not paused to look at the other elements of DCOM®, we would have left the meeting 15 minutes too early, with the management team focusing only on the "D" to e-mail reports in weekly. Had we not backtracked to ensure that everyone had all the resources they needed (the "O" or Opportunity) and the skills they needed to perform this task (the "C" or Competence), Steve still would not have received his weekly reports from everyone.

Step 4: Measure Results and Behaviors

Next, we measure to see if we are achieving the intended changes. We can measure the occurrence of the behavior, or occurrence of the results, or both. They are related but very different things. A behavior change (or no change) can often be seen within a few hours or days, but a results change often takes until the end of the month. Regardless, it is valuable to measure both.

Monitoring behavior creates the opportunity to give employees objective feedback on how they are doing. Feedback shapes their behavior positively and proactively. It also gives us an early (leading) indicator of results.

Frequently reviewing results with all managers is good management practice, but few of our managers actually conducted these reviews. So we explained why reviewing results was important and helped our managers review them until it became natural.

For our locomotive mechanic, tracking repeat failures allows him to see just how many locomotives are returning to the shop. The Mechanical Department can use these data to discuss what worked, what didn't, and what is standing in the way of the team fixing problems right the first time. It will surprise some, but we often see teams rally around decisions that are made to improve the results.

Leaders can be most effective when they measure behavior and results together. Monitoring individual behaviors (and providing personal feedback) while sharing team results in monthly meetings (and addressing barriers) lets the leader spot and address all factors that may be constraining the team.

Monitoring behaviors can be especially helpful—necessary, in fact—where employees are being asked to learn new behaviors to get out of their comfort zone. This is why we monitored behaviors during our culture change.

Step 5: Coach to Drive Desired Behaviors

Last come feedback and coaching, the most powerful tools of all. Good coaching sets clear performance expectations and seeks opportunities to catch people doing it right, as well as when they are not doing it right. Skillful feedback and coaching are hallmarks of truly outstanding leaders. The training and coaching on this step of the ABC Toolkit showed everyone how to give feedback in ways that removed employees' anxiety and fear.

If a leader regularly monitors behavior and reviews results, coaching becomes simple: You coach employees based on what the behavior and results show. This sounds easy, but it takes help to make it happen with precision, and it takes practice to build it into a solid management habit.

PART

V

ALIGNING THE SWITCHES

With a clear vision of the culture we wanted to create, and the tools to do it right, the next step was aligning the switches in the right direction toward change. Aligning the switches required finding sponsorship, testing the business case for the tools, and setting a plan to broaden our efforts.

11

Finding a Champion

As the Q4 Leadership℠ concept began to spread and the success of early executive coaching became evident, executives began to ask, "How can we do this with my team and managers?"

One of those executives was Keith Heller, Senior Vice President of the Eastern Canada Region. Keith is known as a hard-hitter, so perhaps he surprised some with his acute interest in the ABCs. But he is also an eager student of change, always open to new ideas.

As Keith went through coaching himself, he saw opportunities to apply it across his organization. He saw how additional training and coaching would help his leaders either become Q4 leaders or become *better* Q4 leaders.

Keith worked with Hunter, Les Dakens, and Peter Edwards to develop a plan that focused not only on quickly improving performance, but on building a better long-term culture in the Eastern Region.

A Quiet Tryout in Capreol

Richard Sandrock, a veteran CLG consultant, was assigned to the project, for a good reason: He fit. Richard is known for his down-in-the-trenches frontline work in companies and his ability to learn an organization and work collaboratively with both management and union people.

Richard recalls, "Consultants were not popular in CN. We had to prove that CLG's behavioral approach to culture change could work in the railroad environment. So we needed a site for a quiet tryout of the ABCs."

Keith Heller chose the little rail town of Capreol, about 200 miles north of Toronto. Named for an early rail promoter, Capreol remains a small but important rail yard.

Richard tells the story:

> I first met Keith Heller in Montreal, along with Ned Morse and Katrina Kam, a CN manager. I asked Keith why he chose Capreol for our tryout. He replied, "Because I think the people there will give you and the ABCs a chance." As I met people in Capreol, I quickly saw that he was right.
>
> General Manager Tony Marquis was immediately interested in the ABCs because he saw their power to improve safety, his top priority. Head of Engineering Tom Wincheruk, tough-talking and highly respected, bought the ABCs immediately because it brought structure to what he was already trying to achieve.
>
> When you are trying to change a culture, trust is everything. We consultants must have real knowledge of our client's industry and environment. I was new to railroads, so I volunteered to ride the rails with Tom Wincheruk and his team of track supervisors around New Year's, to observe and learn.
>
> Capreol was under glaciers thousands of years ago, and it still feels like it during winter. North of the Great Lakes, it can be bitter, especially in windswept rail yards and along the barren railroad.
>
> For several days, I rode with Tom and his track supervisors in a highrail—a pickup truck outfitted with railroad wheels—inspecting hundreds of miles of rails. They used sophisticated instrumentation and directly observed the track through blowing snow, revealing critical things about the condition of the track:
>
> - Whether the space between the two rails was within spec (rails can shift, leading to derailments, especially in winter).
> - Whether rails were flexing up and down because the gravel ballast underneath had frozen.
> - Whether there were cracks in the rails that could cause them to break or even shatter in the frigid winter.

We slept in bunkhouses alongside the track and dealt with stubborn moose that refused to yield the right of way. Through it all, our mutual respect grew. They saw my genuine interest in them, eagerness to learn how they worked, and unconcern with rank and hierarchy. And I saw their deep professionalism and knowledge and their commitment to providing North America's best rail service.

But shortly after Richard's trip in early 2003, Hunter was promoted to CEO, and he immediately fired all consultants and ordered them off CN's property. In his experience, consultants added little value and cost plenty.

Keith Heller's enthusiasm had grown as he saw what CLG could do for him and his employees. Despite this, Hunter's action left him no choice but to halt the practice run in Capreol. This could have been the end of the fledgling partnership between CN and CLG— but it turned out to be just the beginning.

"I Hate Consultants!"

When Hunter booted the consultants, Les, Peter, and Ned Morse huddled. Progress was being made. The brief experience in Capreol had been just enough to show what CN and CLG could do together to change the culture.

So the three men decided to take their case directly to Hunter. They owed it to him to share their vision of a better way to run the company.

Peter Edwards picks up the story:

> As the three of us waited outside Hunter's office, Les frowned. "We'll get thirty minutes max with him. If it goes south, we'll be lucky to get five." He turned to Ned. "If this meeting fails, CLG's relationship with CN will evaporate, Ned."
>
> So we strode into Hunter's office, masking the shakiness we all felt. At first, Hunter was his usual gracious self, chatting in his disarming Memphis drawl with Ned, whom he had met once before. But as soon as we were seated, he looked Ned straight in the eye.

"Ned, you know I hate consultants. But Les says I should meet with you. So what can you do for me?"

Ned nodded and looked Hunter straight back. "I can save you a ton of money. I'll back that up by putting our fees at risk. If CLG can't save you at least twice what you pay us, then you don't pay us anything."

That got Hunter's attention. "All right, how?"

"By changing the behavior of your people. By changing *how* an engineer maintains the right-of-way so ballast doesn't shift. By changing *how* switches are correctly handled in a yard. By getting better inspection of incoming cars. By getting less dwell time in maintenance, before your cars go back in service."

We had Hunter's attention. But he wanted assurance, so we shared the initial progress that Richard Sandrock and others had made at Capreol.

The meeting survived its first 10 minutes. It looked promising when Hunter asked, "So *how* do you change behavior?"

Hunter Meets the ABCs

Ned took a tablet and wrote three large letters on it: A B C.

He pointed to the B. "Start here. B is for the behaviors that make you money, or lose it. These are the behaviors that get people home safely every night, or send them to the hospital. These are the behaviors I know you care about, because you told me about them when we first met in Chicago."

Ned continued, "A is for antecedents—the things you use every day to trigger those behaviors—things like meetings, memos, policies, procedures, plans, goals, measures, and so on. All that stuff is needed, of course. But it's not enough to keep the behaviors that you want going for long."

Then Ned pointed to the C. "*This is the key.* This is what drives behavior—it's the *consequences* that happen to people for their behavior."

Hunter sat back in his chair. He looked at Les, looked back at Ned, and spread his arms. "That's news to people?! That's the *only* way you get things done! I already know that. That's how I run things. There's a mystery here?"

Ned said, "To you there's no mystery—that's why you have been so successful. But this really is a surprise to many people—

actually, to most people. They may know it intuitively. But they don't know it *consciously*, and don't act on it. Most people don't know how to use consequences effectively."

It's about Culture

"Hunter, this is what cultures are made of. CN's culture is nothing more than a collection of behaviors that have been shaped by consequences over time."

Hunter said, "I agree we need to change the culture. But what makes you so sure we need to teach leaders how to use consequences?"

"Fair question," Ned nodded. "Let me tie culture change to consequences. Most efforts to change things focus on antecedents. Leaders try to launch new behaviors by using antecedents like meetings, policies, new rules, decrees, messages, and ribbon cuttings."

Hunter was expressionless, studying Ned's animated face.

"But these antecedents just don't budge the culture. You know why? Because they don't change what really drives people to perform their best, and that's *consequences.*

"*Culture is all about consequences.* So to answer your question, we define culture like this." He ticked off the points on his fingers—

- Culture is the pattern of behaviors . . .
- that are encouraged or discouraged . . .
- by people and systems . . .
- over time.

"So it's all about consequences, and what people learn will happen for something they do, or don't do. If they expect positive consequences for doing something, then they're more likely to do it. If they expect negative consequences, or none at all, they won't do it. It's really that simple.

"Culture is a result of people's history of what will happen to them when they double-check a coupling, or whether a switch is set properly, or if they miss a damage spot on a car and let it get through. That's culture."

Hunter leaned back and thought for a moment.

Then he started talking about his experience with culture change in a past job with another railroad. He talked about the millions they'd put into culture change, which included nationwide meetings supported by a consulting firm. He called these meetings love fests, saying they even burned incense so people knew something was different. His disdain was clear.

But he saw that this approach was very different. We grew hopeful that Hunter might give our plan a chance.

"What you say makes sense," Hunter said. "But what about the impact on real results? Can you prove it?"

Can You Prove It?

"Hunter, we get real results. We can guarantee a two-to-one return for our work, as long as you and I agree on specific results to target, results that we can measure.

"The challenge is to measure directly what that impact is. At the top, it's very hard. But as we get closer to the front line, it's easier to measure the impact of a change in behavior, because it is at the front line where productivity, quality, and safety are gained or lost."

It became apparent that Hunter would agree to move forward, at least with some pilot work. We wanted agreement on three full-blown pilots, ideally one for each of CN's regions in Eastern Canada, Western Canada, and the United States.

Hunter was thoughtful. "If you really can get me a two-to-one return, it's worth a try. If people want to do this, I'll support it. But the business units will have to pay for it."

Ned and Hunter shook hands, and we started planning the pilots.

CHAPTER 12

Testing the Business Case

Hunter and Ned Morse had agreed to three full-blown pilots of the ABCs, one in each of CN's operating regions in the United States, Eastern Canada, and Western Canada. It was critical to prove quickly that we could help leaders change the culture and get an immediate bump in results. So we sought sites for the pilots that met these requirements:

- A *tough unionized environment*—one where union-management relations had broken down. If we could build leadership skills to improve relations, it would demonstrate that we could make changes in any area of the business.
- *The right size*—small enough so we could fully engage employees, but large enough to show the ABCs would be successful at larger rail yards.
- *The right site leaders*—willing to give the change their best effort.

Each of the three operating regions had its own unique culture and challenges, so we needed to conduct a pilot in each one to show the process would work. Luckily, during the tryout in the Eastern Region and our talks with Hunter, we had gotten interest from the senior vice presidents (SVPs) for the other two regions.

We worked with each SVP to select a site in his region. In the Southern Region, we chose Memphis, Tennessee. In the Canadian West, we picked Transcona, Manitoba, a Winnipeg suburb. And in the Canadian East, we selected Capreol, Ontario—the small town where CLG consultant Richard Sandrock had done the ABCs tryout with encouraging results. We launched the three pilots in 2003.

The first step was to train and coach the leaders in the basics of the ABCs. Leaders had to grasp how antecedents and consequences drive every behavior, including their own. At each site, we partnered a CLG consultant with a CN human resources manager to conduct the training, provide on-site coaching of leaders, and support the leadership team through the change.

We faced a mix of challenges. Some leaders were happy to see us and wondered why it had taken so long for the company to take action. Others were leery, suspecting a flavor-of-the-month program, and unsure they wanted to risk their necks on significant change. And there were many in the middle, hopeful but cautious.

Understandably, leaders wanted to see commitment and results before they would fully engage in the program. Each day, as they observed more results from their training, they believed a little more. Eventually, we achieved a critical mass of believers, and even a few zealots.

The pilots are highly individual stories of drilling down to what really works, what tools to use, and getting it right in each tough environment. The tools and how they are used in a real-life workplace helped us convert abstract ideas into tangible results.

Pilot 1: Partnering in Memphis

The Memphis pilot used an important metric, called *F7*, that indicated how often a repaired locomotive was kicked back within seven days to fix the identical problem. Application of the ABCs quickly cut that rework from a baseline of 12 percent to below 4 percent, better than their goal.

The CLG consultant on this pilot, Russ Ridley, worked with the repair shop manager to improve work processes and change the way employees did the work. What he did *not* do was seat these seasoned railroaders in a classroom and show them PowerPoints on process mapping, continuous improvement, and behavioral theory!

Instead, Russ sat in on management meetings, asking questions and probing to discover why rework was so high. Together, Russ and the shop manager got employees talking about process changes and behavior changes that could reduce the rework. They engaged this group of hard-nosed railroaders in identifying how to improve, and made sure they had the resources and freedom needed to make the changes.

The whole point of successful consulting is to transfer the tools and skills to the client, so the client can continue on its own. That is what Russ did. After helping the team improve on several measures, he began to show them how he was using the ABC Toolkit we had put together to guide their thinking and decision making.

Over time, the team picked up many of these skills. They used them because they worked, because they were common sense, and because we had put a premium on making them easy to use.

In a period of six months, the Memphis repair shop returned remarkable results:

- Repair reliability improved sharply, with locomotive repeat failures dropping 50 percent.
- The length of time railcars were out of service for maintenance dropped 29 percent.
- Trains on time improved 57 percent.
- Weekly overtime hours decreased 25 percent (385 hours to 290 hours).
- Cost improvement from the six-month pilot totaled $1,444,000—from a pilot that cost about $500,000.

Pilot 2: Partnering in Capreol (Northern Ontario)

From the sweltering summer of Memphis to the subzero snows of Capreol is a long distance in climate and culture. But the results from implementing the ABC Toolkit were the same.

Consultant Richard Sandrock partnered with CN's Human Resources Manager Terry Gallagher to conduct the pilot in Capreol. Richard and Terry teamed with Tom Wincheruk and Tony Marquis, the leaders with whom Richard had worked just a few months prior. They were happy to take on the pilot, as the ABC tools fit the natural leadership styles of both Tony and Tom. Both welcomed the help to make significant change. Together, they went about identifying opportunities for improvement, similar to what Russ Ridley had done in Memphis.

The work was in Engineering, with focus on the productivity of improving the quality of tracks and safety. During the time of the pilot, Capreol returned striking results:

- A 27 percent gain in productivity.
- A 19 percent reduction in train travel time.
- An 11 percent gain in average train speed.
- A 60 percent reduction in train delays.
- Cost improvement to CN totaled $2,072,000—again, from a pilot that cost about $500,000.

More important, through the ABCs, many leaders found new ways to work with employees. As one supervisor observed, "People are using the tools. They are becoming pinpointed in articulating exactly what they need. That is removing the need for the screaming, yelling, bellowing, and name-calling that is traditional within railway operations. We are becoming more business-focused and business-oriented, because people are speaking the same language. There is a distinct change already."

Another supervisor noted, "The whole program is about instilling a positive attitude toward tasks, creating a want-to attitude."

Pilot 3: Partnering in Transcona (Winnipeg)

In western Canada, Transcona Shops is one of CN's largest railcar maintenance facilities, employing over 700 people. Transcona has four main shops that specialize in railcars, locomotives, traction motors, and wheels.

The pilots in Memphis and Capreol proved the efficacy of our behavioral approach to culture change. In those pilots, we worked with managers to focus on a few key business opportunities. Transcona proved to be different. There, we focused the ABCs on helping each leader improve the performance of individual employees. CLG consultant Carol Smith partnered with CN's Human Resources Manager Daryll Trask for the Transcona pilot.

The results proved that the ABCs worked equally well at the individual level. We saw improved employee performance that resulted in productivity gains:

- In the welding area, productivity nearly doubled, resulting in a $50,000 impact annually.

- In the wheel repair shop, productivity improved an average of 6 percent for each employee, with an overall 14 percent improvement by shift.
- Improved focus in change-of-shift briefings accumulated a $25,000 annual impact.
- Improved productivity reduced the need for contractors, creating a $50,000 annual impact.
- A single employee who started coming to work on time gained a lost-time equivalent of $1,000 annual impact.

The results of using the ABCs in Transcona were clear not only in operational metrics but also in the impact on leaders, as heard in their comments:

- "There is no stopping him now—he has taken off. He takes more interest in his work and what others are doing. I see it in what he says and in his e-mails."
- "We've made a lot of changes, but we wouldn't be where we are today without the ABCs."

Learnings from the Pilots

For CN as a company to adopt the ABC tools, the tools had to prove themselves in the pilots. Having success in using them to solve tough current problems meant that leaders would trust them and use them in the future. The pilots showed us how to make the tools most useful in the railroad environment.

Our learnings from the pilots and cultural initiatives in other large organizations distilled down to three critical facts:

1. If the ABCs became a corporate-level mandate and thus were pushed on everyone, it could kill the initiative. The ABCs would be discounted and irrelevant at the supervisor level, and supervisors would simply ride it out as a flavor-of-the-month gimmick until it went away. The only way to spread use of these tools was to ensure they added value so the organization *wanted* and requested them.
2. If we lacked sponsorship from key executives in each operating area, it would be the kiss of death. We needed to work with each executive, learning what would be most valuable and adjusting training to meet his needs.

3. If we did not offer leaders high-touch, shoulder-to-shoulder support to ensure that they would act to change our culture, it would not happen. We needed to continue the on-site, 24/7 coaching that made the pilots so successful.

We Did What We Said We Would Do

After six months, we prepared our results for Hunter. The pilots were a combined effort, so we decided to present results at Hunter's executive team meeting, which included the SVPs for the three regions. Each presented the results of his pilot.

In our results, we looked for three indicators of success:

1. Did we see leaders applying the ABCs to performance opportunities as a new way to lead their teams?
2. Did we see changes in employee behavior that were early indicators of movement in the culture?
3. Did we see improved business results as a result of these changes?

The finance department helped quantify the improvements we were seeing. A good example was locomotive downtime. Finance said that having a locomotive off-line for a day cost the company a certain number of dollars. We compared that figure to the increased availability of locomotives that were not returned for rework, and came up with 67 percent savings.

We ran similar analyses for all the results we had achieved. We compared those savings to the amount we'd invested in these pilots (primarily CLG's consulting fees) and determined the return on investment (ROI).

Ned Morse had promised at least a 200 percent return on investment. In two of the three pilots, we had clear business results demonstrating at least what he had promised: a 12-month ROI of 290 percent in the United States (Memphis) and 296 percent in the Eastern Region (Capreol).

Further, these improvements impacted the Five Guiding Principles:

- In Memphis, the ABCs improved locomotive availability (Service, Asset Utilization, Cost Control).

- In Capreol, the ABCs improved the quality of CN's tracks and right-of-way (Service, Asset Utilization, Cost Control, Safety).

These results meant fewer delays, improved train speeds, and improved on-time performance overall, yielding genuine economic advantages.

In Transcona, the pilot focused on helping leaders address performance improvement for individual employees, so the results did not show direct ROI improvements like the other pilots. They resulted in a modest ROI, but with far more valuable results in the cultural improvements.

The pilots demonstrated an overall ROI of 3.21:1 (321 percent) over a 12-month period. But, because we hit our goal of 2:1 return in only two out of three, CLG dutifully waived its $300,000 fee for Transcona, as promised. This waiver startled veterans at CN. To them it was a big sign that CLG was serious and not your run-of-the-mill consultancy.

Although the bottom-line results didn't happen at Transcona, there was remarkable individual development and the start of culture change. This showed a longer-term value-add and not just a blip on the radar. It was a fundamental change, and CN wanted more.

Clearly it wasn't just about the numbers. It was also about leadership and changes in day-to-day behaviors. The measurable results were impressive, but there were even more anecdotes about how the work had changed an individual or a rail yard. The real value was in the new *tone* we created—the *culture*.

Just as important was the highly favorable response to the culture change and performance improvement we observed in employees at all levels who were normally consultant-averse. It wasn't just a few groups—it was unionized rank-and-file, first-line supervisors, second-level leaders (superintendents, shift leaders, etc.), area managers, general managers, district VPs, and the three regional SVPs.

A Skeptical Hunter Gives the Nod

After we presented our results, we could see that Hunter was bothered. He looked around at his senior team. Then he returned to the point he had made at our very first meeting: "This is not rocket science. It's all about consequences. How come our people aren't doing this all the time? Do we need some damn consultant to run the business?"

The room chilled. His executives couldn't argue with Hunter's logic: *We shouldn't have to train our leaders in the basics.* But the reality that they had seen with their own eyes was that we *did* need to do just that. Many leaders lacked the skills to lead effectively, and now they had the tools to help them. As the team thought fast for a diplomatic way to break this news, Ned chimed in.

"Hunter, here's a rule of thumb: Roughly 15 percent of a normal management population understands how to do these things naturally. Clearly, you are in that 15 percent, and likely so are many others in this room. Managing through consequences is second nature to you.

"But about 85 percent of managers don't get this. Especially as you get closer to the front line, this is *not* second nature to people. They simply need help in learning how to lead."

A number of the SVPs weighed in to Hunter. Like him, they were hard-as-nails railroaders, but they clearly saw the value here. They saw what many of our leaders had been missing. This recognition swayed Hunter's opinion, and we got the nod to proceed *if* the SVPs of his three regions wanted it. He viewed it as their decision to make for their respective operations.

And so we began planning how to create large-scale change across the entire organization.

13

Gaining Visible Sponsorship: The CEO's Essential Role

Hunter's support for using the ABCs to develop CN's leadership was no surprise to those who know him well. Even prior to CLG's arrival, he had taken two major steps toward defining leadership at CN: his authorship of a book that presents CN's operating principles to all CN employees, and his creation of "Hunter Camps" to develop leaders.

These are actions that any CEO can take in any company.

"How We Work and Why"

Hunter's first act of sponsorship was to document his Five Guiding Principles.

While they only took a moment to scribble: Service, Cost Control, Asset Utilization, Safety, People—writing down how to actually apply them, with examples that would teach people—that was another project, a much bigger one.

The work already under way was part of demonstrating Hunter's sponsorship for the culture change. At first, we planned just a few pages to document and clarify the Five Guiding Principles. But as we worked on our deployment plan, we realized that all employees, top to bottom, needed to understand our business drivers, *how* Hunter expected us to work under the Five Guiding Principles, and *why* we were so committed to them.

We saw the power in the stories that Hunter employed to communicate the Five Guiding Principles to people face-to-face, so we added them. The pages multiplied. Soon a few pages became a 146-page hardcover book published in full color and in three languages, filled with stories from the field! It had a title that most people found odd at first, but now seems ingenious in its simplicity: *How We Work and Why.*

It was a simple, heartfelt, often blunt statement of what CN is about. *How We Work and Why* is about our Five Guiding Principles and how we use them to manage ourselves and make our railway the best. (See Figure 13.1.)

In 2005, everybody in CN was sent a copy—all 22,500 employees. It was one of Hunter's ways of showing how serious he was about the changes we were starting to make across all of CN. He wanted everyone to know just exactly what he expected from people and why.

But the book was also a very concrete way to spotlight our many positive leaders spread across CN. The book is filled with *their* stories, with *their* examples of personally leading in the new way. No stories from negative leaders found their way into this book.

We had yet another motive behind the book: to show people that the changes we wanted to make were already under way in many parts of the company, and that what we envisioned was very doable. As one person put it, "This book tells me that the train has already left the station!"

Indeed it had—and *How We Work and Why* helped demonstrate Hunter's visible sponsorship for spreading the engagement that already existed in parts of CN across the entire company. The book became our main vehicle for communicating our vision, mission, and plan to get there.

Did we keep the book a closely held corporate secret, stamped "Company Confidential?" No, we freely shared it. *How We Work and Why* offers models, like our Five Guiding Principles and Precision Railroading, that anyone is welcome to adopt. Those are not our secret, and we'd like to see other organizations use them so all business can run better. Our real secret lies in hiring extraordinary leaders who use the power of Q4 Leadership[SM], combined with the ABCs, to hit our results targets.

It wasn't long before others sought copies of the book: CEOs of other major railways, mayors of major cities, customers, government departments, and people in completely different businesses. People wanted to know what we were about and how we get our results.

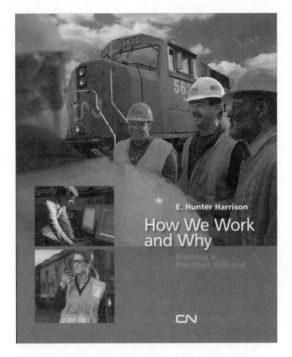

Figure 13.1   Hunter Harrison's *How We Work and Why*

Source: E. Hunter Harrison, *How We Work and Why*, © 2005 Canadian National Railway Company.

We even received requests from a number of companies and government departments in China for an edition in Mandarin, which we gladly provided!

Addressing the Naysayers

Most readers gave *How We Work and Why* a very positive response. Employees from across CN wrote to Hunter, saying, "I get it."

Of course, not everyone got it. A few who hadn't liked the culture change of the past few years, or who didn't believe that Hunter was serious about the new culture, took the opportunity to tell him in writing.

In many companies, such negative letters would have been brushed off or replied to politely by some staffer. But that was not what the new CN nor Hunter was about. Detesting paperwork and bureaucracy, Hunter would do what he became famous for: He would grab the phone, call the employee, and discuss it.

If the letter was a thoughtful response to his book, Hunter would listen to the employee's views. Almost always, these people wanted his vision to succeed—they were just dubious that it could really happen. Hunter would end up asking for their help in getting the changes put in place—the changes they both wanted.

If the letter was a negative screed, Hunter would challenge the employee to defend his or her position. There were sparks at times—but it was no longer an unhappy employee flinging mud toward an anonymous corporation. It was now person-to-person, one-on-one—with the CEO himself!

By personally talking to employees like this, Hunter convinced a lot of people to give the new culture a chance. More important, he started a new leadership trend. As word spread, other leaders began to take the same tactic—they simply picked up the phone and called.

CHAPTER 14

Learning from a Strike

Our blissful excitement about changing the culture following the pilots and getting Hunter's support didn't last long. Shortly after we began planning to take the ABCs companywide, we ran straight into a strike of CN's 4,500 employees represented by the Canadian Auto Workers (CAW). These employees, including mechanics and clerks, represented about 20 percent of CN's workforce.

The CAW's executives had approved the deal and unanimously recommended it to their members. The union's web site said it was one of the best wage-and-benefit agreements out there. Both sides had to ask themselves: Why and over what?

It helps to know that many of the CAW members didn't vote at all, either for or against the agreement. The result was that the minority who did vote for a strike tipped the scales by a slim percentage. Thus, a small minority of the membership took the whole group out on strike.

In the past, the company simply would have offered more cash or benefits to avoid a strike, reflecting CN's old culture of acceptance, early quits, and such. But we were changing the culture now, and would no longer take the easy way out. The CAW agreement was a critical switchpoint—an opportunity to spike the switch for the future.

We had worked with the CAW's leaders to reach a resolution but could not get to yes. This was partly because of our history with the unions: When they turned down a deal, we would eventually relent.

But this time we didn't. It was a fair deal, their executives had agreed to it, and we couldn't walk away—so we took a strike. As we changed our culture, it was a tough but necessary spiking of the switch.

Spiking the Switch

The spike came in the form of an impassioned letter Hunter sent to all CAW members the day before the strike deadline. It came straight from his heart, and employees talk about it to this day:

> TO ALL CN EMPLOYEES REPRESENTED BY THE CAW:
>
> I am writing to share my thoughts with you. I'm a no-nonsense and straightforward guy who values people. Nobody appreciates a good loyal railroader more than me. I have worked in the shops and know the great work you provide to CN. Together with the CAW, we have accomplished a lot in the last few years, including in-sourcing to Transcona, adding clerical work to Canada, creating new jobs at Auto-ramp & Cargo-Flo, and hiring shopcraft apprentices, mechanics, and clerks.
>
> As your CEO, I need to represent three groups: customers, employees, and shareholders. During the recent negotiations, we felt our offer to you was a fair package and it was supported by your union representatives. I have been told that the deal was rejected for several reasons, including how CN is disciplining employees. We have looked at the last 18 months of discipline records, and we have learned that about 1 percent of the 5,000 CAW employees have received a suspension or discharge during that time. The Union has brought to our attention that we may have been heavy-handed in certain cases. I want to assure you that we are discussing each case with your union representatives.
>
> We just want a good job from every CN employee. On the wage issue, I must tell you, as I told your union leaders, our total package was very fair and we have been consistent that the overall cost of the settlement will not be increased.
>
> So, where does this leave us now? You do have the right to strike to achieve your goals. We have the right to continue to service our customers and prevent a financial loss to our shareholders. Since I am very passionate about the railroad

business, I hope you recognize I will take whatever action is necessary to continue running the railroad during a strike action.

Unfortunately, as we know from watching past strikes in the railroad industry, nobody wins, and our relationship will be damaged for a long time.

All I ask of each of you is to reflect on what we have together at CN. We in management are not perfect—we want to get better. We all love this company, so let's work together to fix our problems.

Thank you.

E. Hunter Harrison,
President and CEO

Straightforward as his letter was, it was not enough, and the strike began. During the month-long walkout, the 4,500 mechanics and clerks were temporarily replaced by about 2,000 managers. We gave the managers the necessary training and put them on the job. They learned how to repair railcars and locomotive engines, to invoice customers, and to process paychecks.

Accountants and lawyers became crane operators and lift truck specialists. We saw IT managers become excellent customer service representatives, because they understood the systems used to input orders. Indeed, their familiarity with our systems enabled them to suggest process improvements once the strike was over.

Through the strike, our managers gained a greater appreciation for the work needed to keep the railroad running. They also developed ideas to streamline processes, make jobs easier, and run the organization more efficiently.

Start with the Supervisors

After the CAW strike, Hunter spoke. "Look—what caused this strike shows us that neither the union executives nor we knew what was going to happen. We don't know our people well enough, and they certainly don't understand what we're about. We've got to get our supervisors trained—start there."

First-line supervisors have the hardest job in any company. Upper levels of management push their demands down, and line employees push their demands up, catching first-line supervisors in the middle.

Most of our first-line supervisors have come up through the union ranks. CN works hard to make sure that candidates for first-line supervisor are a good fit with the job's requirements. When an up-through-the-ranks supervisor is trained properly and has the right leadership acumen, we believe there is no better person to drive results.

Study after study confirms that people will stay with or leave a company because of their direct supervisor, who for most employees is their interface with the company. How this person chooses to lead shapes the employees' performance and beliefs about the organization. We needed Q4 leaders throughout. Employees rely on first-line supervisors for *direction, competence* (through training), the *opportunity* to do their best, and the *motivation* to give it their all—the four elements of the DCOM® Model. It is part of what our Q4 leaders do. (Chapters 10 and 17 show how DCOM® works.) Employees see their supervisor as the most important person in communicating with them about the company, and they need to fully trust this individual.

Becoming a supervisor at CN carries a special risk: In some groups, newly promoted supervisors have only one year (under union rules) to discover whether the role is right for them. If they wait beyond that year to decide, the union contract says they can't return to the union ranks. This would mean unemployment if they eventually decide that being a supervisor is not for them.

For young workers that might not be so bad. But CN's typical unionized employees are in their late 40s, and some already have 30 years of tenure, which they do not want to put at risk. Not surprisingly, the first-line supervisor job is difficult to fill.

To make matters worse, most of our first-line supervisors had been thrust into their roles with little training in how to manage a tough crowd. The strike revealed that most of them didn't really know how to lead effectively.

While they knew many individuals, they didn't know their assembled teams well enough. Although they effectively directed day-to-day work, many didn't see the bigger picture. So they didn't see the strike coming or understand why employees walked out. For those who did see the strike looming, organizational mud prevented the message from getting to the right ears.

The strike experience confirmed the importance of how first-line supervisors behave with their teams. In the past, the best leaders rallied employees, both before and after strikes. The worst leaders antagonized employees, both before and after strikes. Looking across the organization, we saw both types of leaders at work.

Since the CAW strike involved railroad mechanics, we began by training supervisors in the Mechanical Department of our Canadian operations. In the United States, there was not the same strike-driven need, so we began training by location instead of by department. At each U.S. site, we trained first-line supervisors in groups that included people from the railroad's major functions— Mechanical, Operations, and Engineering.

Several supervisors didn't progress past the training. Once they saw the new and different expectations of Q4 Leadership[SM], they decided it was not for them. Holding people accountable for results and balancing positive and constructive feedback were not what they had signed up for. So some chose to move back into the union ranks, some retired, and we asked others to move on when we saw they couldn't lead in the way we needed.

When you work with supervisors whom you know well, it's really tough to see them fail. For those who couldn't handle the role, we did our best to find other jobs in CN for which they were better suited. After all, most were solid railroaders, experienced in the rail culture. We didn't want to lose them and couldn't see them fail.

Fortunately, the leaders who failed were few. Most successfully completed the training and began working toward Q4 Leadership[SM]. They went on to eliminate many day-to-day issues that had been background causes of the strike.

CHAPTER 15

Planning the Trip

With the CAW strike behind us, we leaped at the opportunity to address the leadership gap highlighted by the walkout. When you know where you want to go and clearly communicate it, a lot of things line up. We eagerly returned to our ABC rollout.

We had very modest funding from CN Corporate, but this was intentional and actually worked in our favor. When new programs are paid for by headquarters, you typically see willingness to come along for the ride (because someone else is paying), lower commitment (it's someone else's money), and headquarters' desire to dictate every step and process.

We avoided much of this by making our mandate that each regional senior vice president own and drive the rollout.

Going to Rome (and Paying for It)

We called our rollout plan "Going to Rome," a play on the saying "All roads lead to Rome." Each group was starting from a different point, moving at its own speed, using varied routes and methods, but we all had the same destination. As we got closer to "Rome," our approaches would grow closer together.

For greatest impact, the enterprise rollout began with the major regional operating groups, not with staff. We knew that if we could demonstrate value to the operating groups, which are the heartbeat of CN, the rest of the company would eventually buy in. Starting with staff groups would have much less impact—Operations was the place to start.

Our initial offer to the three operating regions was for six months of CLG's help with the ABCs, paid for by Hunter through our Human Resources group. After that, if a region wanted to continue with the ABCs, they would have to pick up most of the ongoing costs.

The regions were equally clear on their side that they were willing to expand beyond the pilots done in their region, but would not commit beyond the initial six-month deployment. They wanted a way out in case a broader deployment disturbed their operations.

The first six months flew by, and the impact became evident early. The big early achievements were locomotive rework reduction ("Pilot 1: Partnering in Memphis" in Chapter 12), "Dressed & Ready" (Chapter 18), and on-time train departure ("The ABCs Improve ETAs" in Chapter 19).

Implementing the ABCs CN-Wide

Our journey would take multiple years, but in CN's world this initiative had to prove itself quarter by quarter, project by project. Moving beyond the pilot stage required hard results as we rolled out the ABCs to the many sites in each region. This need for proof of concept actually helped our progress by allowing us to balance resources and leverage success from other areas as we went.

In each region, we created a team to support the rollout. Each worked from the same training script, but customized it for the local audience.

In each region, the process was the same:

- *Training.* Trainers cascaded the rollout of a three-day working session to help leaders get started. Topics included the case for change, the Five Guiding Principles, the ABC Toolkit, and plenty of time to plan and practice the change they intended to make. For maximum effectiveness, we did two days of classroom, followed by some "soak and practice" time, and concluded on the third day.
- *Coaching.* Coaches provided individualized and team coaching to help the tools come to life and help leaders become fluent in using them.
- *Metrics review and discussion.* Leaders reviewed their progress against results and determined what to do differently to improve performance long-term.

The key difference from most training events was that, at the end of the session, we didn't pack up and leave. In the past, many training sessions pretty much went like this: "Here's what you need to know, how you should do it, and good luck." Instead, CLG and CN's Human Resources people stuck around after training to offer leaders coaching support. The coaches embedded themselves in the leadership team, becoming regulars. This allowed them to provide in-the-moment coaching and support to deal with the most challenging issues.

The training sessions were intense. We had only three days to make initial believers out of frontline managers. They had seen too many so-called improvement programs fizzle and too many consultants who actually made things worse and wasted time. We explained the "why" and "what was in it for them" for leaders, employees, and all of CN.

As we worked our way across the organization, we found that some leaders took to the ABCs immediately, while others took longer to adjust their leadership style to fit the new culture.

Selling the ABCs to the Operating Regions

"Dressed & Ready" (described in Chapter 18) was a broad-scale change that simply got employees to suit-up and be ready to start work on time, instead of the customary 15 to 25 minutes late. That doesn't sound like much, but when multiplied across all of CN's people, Dressed & Ready resulted in a 2 percent productivity improvement.

Dressed & Ready should have been a shining example of our progress. Indeed, it was to those who were close to it. Nonetheless, it was the solution to a problem that no one in leadership wanted to admit even existed.

Now came the true test: Corporate funding for on-site coaches began shrinking toward zero. It would now be up to the regions to continue funding of our work. Fortunately, every region leader and their management teams had experienced the business and cultural benefits of the behavioral work led by CLG's consultants.

The regional SVPs now deemed the ABCs essential to achieving the significant performance gains required by the corporate plan. So they voted with their budget dollars, intensifying the coaching, broadening the scope, and accelerating the pace of change.

Indeed, we had to balance the pull for services coming from the regions with other demands that were starting to come from other groups. Our strategy was working!

Occasionally, we needed to nudge a leader to give the ABCs a chance. But more often, leaders would observe behaviors changing and see results improve—which made them hunger for more.

I Love Your Passion, But . . .

Occasionally, there was the risk of an overeager leader getting carried away. It's like the old rule about grocery shopping: Never do it when you are hungry! That's what happened with one of our senior executives, in this story from Peter Edwards:

> The rollout was going well. There were the usual hiccups, but the excitement and results grew daily. I thought I could take a week off with my family in someplace sunny and hot.
>
> Then, the day before we were to leave, I received a voice mail from a senior executive who I will call "Bill."
>
> "Peter!" he exclaimed excitedly. "I'm going to radically step up my group's commitment to the ABCs. I want to get the big bang right now. I told Ned Morse at CLG that I want another 17 consultants immediately. I want them on the ground next week!"
>
> I was delighted that he was seeing the value—but 17 more consultants in his area alone, and immediately? This was too much, too soon.
>
> Faster than I'd thought possible, we had reached the transition from change based on "have to" to "want to!"
>
> I called Ned and he confirmed my concerns. "Of course, we're glad to have the business," he said. "But my advice is not to go this way right now. It's moving too fast."
>
> I cringed. Now I had the unenviable task of asking a senior leader to back off from what we'd asked him to do.
>
> Bill and I traded messages but couldn't connect. Then I saw that he would pass through Toronto when my family and I were leaving. We managed to meet while we awaited our 4:00 A.M. flight. We perched on chairs in the hotel lobby and debated.
>
> "Look, Peter," he said. "I can do whatever I want here. It's my decision, not yours."

"You're right, Bill. But I still get to make one decision."

"What's that?"

"Which newspaper to advertise your job in."

"What?"

"Look, I'm glad you're so enthused," I said. "But neither CLG, nor Les, nor myself think you can integrate 17 consultants into your area at one shot. It is too much, too fast. You're going to blow a lot of money with not enough to show for it."

Then I added, "Bill, people will look at that and think 'Hmm, Bill's judgment is pretty bad,' and then, as the HR guy, I'll be looking for your replacement. Too bad, because I think you're a pretty good guy, and too bad because there's a better way to do this."

Bill gazed out the lobby window into the predawn darkness for a full minute. "Okay, what can we do?"

Then we worked out a plan to increase the number of consultants as we progressed, rather than all at once. Some were to be CLG coaches, and the rest would be CN internal coaches.

It's great to have true believers, but if they get ahead of what the organization can handle, they can be as much of a problem as early skeptics. We had to make sure that our leaders didn't get so far ahead that no one was following!

Managing the Pull

In our rollout plan leading to Rome, the roads were all different. Each region had its own starting place and initial focus. However, they shared three core elements:

1. A strong case for making the change.
2. CN's Five Guiding Principles.
3. The ABC methodology and tools.

We continued our minimalist approach with each new group that wanted to try. In each case, we would train their management group, using people from CN and CLG to explain the case for change and the basic ABC tools.

We then supported this training with up to six months of CLG coaching on the corporate tab. Over time, the CLG coaches were supplemented by some of CN's HR, functional, and operational people who became internal coaches, fully certified to conduct the training and coaching.

This process worked fairly well, allowing us to adjust the training to add the greatest value to each group.

Deployment Wasn't All Rosy

Deploying the ABCs wasn't all rosy, however. We didn't get pull from everywhere. And it wasn't always resistance to change—we made mistakes ourselves.

Judy Johnson tells about one of our missteps, recalling our entrance into CN's Information Technology department. It demonstrates the importance of always understanding exactly where a group is and finding the best approach to help.

> Fred Grigsby, CN's Chief Information Officer, is compassionate and gracious. But at times he can be very passionate and will take no prisoners. Our first meeting went just like that.
>
> Fred had heard about our progress in the operating regions. He was eager to learn how he might use the ABCs to further the improvements he was making in IT.
>
> Our work in the operating regions had given us a formula for success: Train all the leaders in the region (executive through first-line) and follow up with coaching for every leader. That formula was effective at both changing behavior and getting results, plus it was well received by the field.
>
> In the glow of that success, we lost sight of the fact that the formula must always grow from a clearly understood need, not the other way around.
>
> Fred's IT Department wasn't broken. In fact, in his many years as CIO, he had made remarkable strides, leading to being honored as Canada's CIO of the year. He knew there was more to do, and was interested in the potential of the ABCs to help.
>
> But when we talked about rolling out the ABCs, we made a key mistake: We offered Fred the same formula that had succeeded in Operations, instead of fully exploring what he wanted and needed. Bad move.
>
> He didn't buy it. He expected us to recognize his unique culture and needs, and was offended that we simply offered a

formula instead of a solution customized to his needs. He grew quite passionate about our misstep.

We had been asleep at the switch. By not staying true to the customized, built-to-your-needs plan that had made the ABCs so successful in Operations, we inadvertently converted an eager customer into an unhappy opponent.

It took six months and several conversations to truly understand how the culture change could further Fred's goals in IT. After many discussions among the trio of Fred, Peter, and Judy, we finally agreed that one CLG consultant, working with two CN Human Resources managers, would get things going.

CHAPTER

16

Making the Case for Change

We railroaders are practical people, because we have to be. We move heavy cargo thousands of miles, on time, through all manner of changing weather and rail conditions, using giant equipment and perhaps the most far-flung infrastructure of any industry—one where every inch of rail, every signal light, and every switch has to be in good repair 24/7.

We have little time for hypothetical philosophizing or dreamy idealism. We simply have to make it work 24/7, or, as they say, just do it.

So if a tool helps us run the railroad better, we are quick to adopt it. If not, we are quick to reject it. The interval during which we make that decision is very, very short. This is the skeptical environment into which we introduced the ABCs.

The Case for the ABCs

Part of the challenge of changing our culture was to quickly show employees the case for change and that the new ABC tools would work.

We created ways to teach the ABCs that made them come to life and enabled employees to apply them immediately. To spread the message CN-wide, we conducted over 100 workshops, with 15 to 20 leaders at a time. These workshops gave leaders a fresh way of thinking about our business and a set of tools with which to lead more effectively. Every workshop opened by sharing the need for change and stories of how other companies have capitalized on their own need to change.

Peter Edwards recounts a key story used to make the case for change:

> Ice cream was largely a commodity until Häagen-Dazs® created a mass-market, high-quality, super premium-priced product that people gladly pay for.
>
> Prior to that, except for a few regional brands, ice cream was pretty much a perfect commodity. It was the loss leader that every supermarket used to draw you into their stores. It was usually Neapolitan—red, brown, and white. It may have been advertised as strawberry, chocolate, and vanilla, but it certainly didn't taste like any of them. In fact, the list of ingredients started to look like one of the better chemistry sets as additives replaced cream and milk.
>
> Häagen-Dazs® changed all this with its super premium ice cream with a super premium price.
>
> They are innovating constantly. From the initial few choices, they now offer over 39 flavors of ice cream and over nine varieties on a stick. They have National Flavor Search contests and special limited edition ice creams! They understand that innovation is what keeps them distinct from their competitors.
>
> They are not alone. Now consider automobiles. At one time, Japanese automobiles were synonymous with poor design and even worse quality. Now, Toyota has become the fastest-growing auto manufacturer in the United States.
>
> Despite this success, Toyota was determined to conquer new markets. They decided that they would enter the high-margin, premium-car category because that's where the richest profits are. Critics and analysts said they were crazy. The world had more than enough high-end automobiles.
>
> Toyota didn't listen to the conventional wisdom, and an unlikely-named "Lexus" was born. Now Lexus has established itself as a standard of luxury. Its vehicles compete with the best in the world.
>
> Will this market dominance continue? Only if Toyota continues to embrace change and improve. There are many companies ready to challenge them in the future. In fact, innovation continues to create competition. GM's hybrid Volt could entirely change the world's perception of what an automobile can be.

These stories illustrate that you don't have a choice around change. If you decide not to change, the world will change around you.

In the workshops, employees related these stories to the progress they had witnessed on their own jobs at CN. They also knew that opportunities to improve remained abundant.

Our leaders and employees had already been through a lot of change as we worked our way to become the number one railroad in North America. We acquired that distinction the old-fashioned way—we earned it. People were a bit weary, however, so we knew selling the need for still further change would be tough.

Spreading the Word

This is where the commitment of CN's leaders shone. It was tough scheduling them, because you obviously cannot just stop a railroad while you work on your culture. But culture change was a priority, so they made the time. The commitment was so strong that one manager presented five times in one week, each in a different time zone (Canada has six).

Executives, local leaders, Human Resource partners, and CLG consultants worked together to kick off every workshop. These workshops were critical, not only to teach leaders new skills but to engage them in the change. We did three things to set up the workshops for success:

1. *We explained the case for change.* Having people understand *why* we needed to change was (and always is) the key to acceptance. This case was presented by the site leader to help people grasp why the railway had to keep getting even better, despite having already gone from good to great.
2. *We integrated the Five Guiding Principles into the first day of each workshop as "Here is what we need to do."* Then we presented the ABC principles and *how* to implement them.
3. *We combined CN and CLG resources to facilitate each workshop.* When people see local leaders willing to champion the cause, and their local Human Resources person is knowledgeable and ready to help, and an external partner is working side-by-side with them to lend their expertise in very practical

ways—they understand that it is a well-thought-out effort with serious commitment from the top.

Answering Four Basic Questions

Once everyone was committed, the stage was set for change to become effective. There were no guarantees; many other things also needed to happen. But without everyone's commitment, what was assured was failure.

To get employee commitment, we answered four basic questions that we knew were high in the minds of every CN employee.

Question 1: Why Do We Have to Change?

CN was not losing market share, nor were competitors passing us by. We were doing so well that some thought, why change?

Well, change we must, because in any business it's not just about being the best. To get a premium for what we do, our customers must see a significant, measurable difference between us and the competition—a differentiator that is useful to them and justifies our rates.

Think what has happened in the airline industry. Over time, their service and points of differentiation have dropped. To most people, all airlines are the same. This is why price has become such a big differentiator and why airlines are generally treated as commodities. You won't pay extra for one versus another, because you don't think the experience will justify the price.

At CN, this state of affairs was part of our past, and we didn't want it to be our future. We needed to go further because our strategy was to do something no railroad had ever attempted before: Differentiate ourselves on the quality of our service so we could escape the historical commodity pricing that had characterized our industry for decades.

We wanted to provide a premium service to those who wanted it, in return for premium rates. Premium service justifies premium rates, which bring premium revenue, which brings industry-leading margins that reward shareholders, leaders, and employees alike. We can charge a premium only when our customers see a significant, measurable competitive difference in our service that is truly important to them.

Question 2: What Does the Future Look Like?

Our vision is to build a company that continuously drives premium service and differentiates itself from the competition over the long run. As a result, our employees and shareholders will benefit. We know the only way to do this is through the single differentiator that is unique to CN—our people. Our future is every employee, fully engaged, committed in the vision, and recognized for the results.

Question 3: What's My Part?

Employees must understand their role in a change. If they don't, they can't adapt, causing needless stress. Changing our culture depended on the support and involvement of every employee across every region at every level. They not only needed to understand the change we were undertaking; they needed to own it.

That's why we asked local leaders to participate in our workshops. They were in the best position to explain the change and the role of each employee in its success.

Question 4: WIIFM? (What's in It for Me?)

This is one of the most important parts of creating change. You can answer the preceding three questions, but *if there is no clear WIIFM, people won't change.*

It's obvious in our personal lives. When you already own an oven, why buy a microwave? Because what's in it for you is that it's faster and easier, and your life becomes simpler.

In the workplace, it is not always so obvious. Will it make my job easier or harder? More interesting or boring? Overall better, or more complex, tedious, or bureaucratic?

This isn't just selfish. Employees do many things selflessly, for the good of others. But for a major change in anyone's daily routine, it sure helps to clearly see a benefit to ourselves and our families.

CHAPTER

17

Expanding Sponsorship

The CEO's sponsorship of an enterprise-wide change is essential, but it is not enough. Sponsorship must cascade down level by level, and it needs to do so at the same time changes are taking root from the bottom up.

Fortunately for us, the senior vice presidents were more than willing to sponsor the culture change. In fact, we didn't even have to encourage them—they were leading people and committing resources on their own. Each leader built his own plan and way of making it visible in his organization. Each took a unique approach that fit his personality, situation, and the type of leaders below him.

In this chapter, we highlight three examples of visible leadership:

- *Visiting sites to set the stage*—Gordon Trafton, Senior Vice President, Southern Region.
- *Sponsoring a safety-first culture*—Keith Creel, Senior Vice President, Eastern Canada Region.
- *Personally walking the talk*—Claude Mongeau, Chief Financial Officer.

Example 1: Visiting Sites to Set the Stage

Gordon Trafton is SVP of CN's Southern Region, which spans from New Orleans to Winnipeg and includes three major acquisitions: the Illinois Central Railroad (approved in 1999), Wisconsin Central (2001), and Great Lakes Transportation (2004). When Hunter asked Gordon to sponsor the culture change work in his region, Gordon immediately wanted to deploy the plan, tools, and processes we had developed. As he put it:

> We had three legacy cultures here—CN, the Illinois Central, and the Wisconsin Central. [The Great Lakes Transportation acquisition had not yet happened.] We needed to develop a single CN culture, and this was the way to do it.
>
> But more deeply, I have seen what our people can do when we tap their Discretionary Performance℠ by creating a culture of engagement. I have seen the places where our positive leaders are out in front and set the tone for their workplace, making great places to work.
>
> I've also seen places where negative leaders are kings of the hill, and they are terrible places to work—unsafe, high turnover, poor productivity, problems constantly simmering between the rank-and-file and management. If you're an upbeat, can-do person, why would you want to go to work and face that environment every day?
>
> I wanted every terminal, customer service office, yard, and engineering shop in my region to be a great place in which to work. The ABCs gave us the tools to accomplish this.

From his predecessor, Gordon inherited one of the three original ABC pilots—Memphis. When he came on board, he reviewed the data from that pilot (Chapter 12) and made time to talk with many of the people involved. He liked what he heard. But it was the science behind the work that fully convinced him the ABCs would help him lead his region.

Visible Sponsorship

Gordon started to visit the many workplaces under his charge. Doing so took many days spread over several months. He went to talk *with* the employees in his region, and not *to* them.

In a typical meeting, he communicated with them:

> This is my vision for how great workplaces should perform and what it should be like to work in them. Great workplaces have—
>
> - Highly visible data.
> - Frequent feedback about performance.
> - People engaged in solving performance problems.
> - High levels of recognition for those deserving it.

- Equally high levels of developmental feedback for those needing to improve.
- A feeling of being valued and important to the whole organization.
- A sense of working with a really great team.

Creating such a workplace depends on leadership—which I define as much more encompassing than our managers and supervisors. I appeal to the leadership potential inside each of you—your potential to help lead the cultural changes needed to make your workplace great.

Gordon also delivered a wake-up call to negative leaders to get with the program and a mandate to positive leaders to take charge. On a flipchart, he would sketch the Spectrum of Employee Engagement (Chapter 4), then ask everyone, "Where are you on this spectrum?" He urged the neutral majority to "get out of the stands and onto the playing field—we need you."

Gordon would then shift the meeting into an extremely candid dialogue among employees who cared deeply about their railroad. There was debate, challenge, emotion, and strong viewpoints. But with these meetings, he:

- Demonstrated sponsorship for the upcoming culture change initiatives.
- Helped employees understand the "why" for these changes from CN's perspective.
- Showed why the changes fit his own values and view of what good leaders should be doing.
- Explained what was in it for the employees themselves.

Modeling Good Leadership

Gordon modeled what he believed good leaders should do: He talked with people, listened, and spoke candidly. He shared data that most had never seen before—data about their costs, their unit's reliability, their productivity in relation to other units. He asked for their ideas on improving the performance underlying this data. He listened intently to their views on what was needed to unlock their Discretionary Performance^{SM}.

After visiting each site, he continued modeling good leadership by rapidly following through on the many ideas that each visit surfaced, so employees saw action. Gordon worked through the local management team. He wanted to demonstrate how to take people's ideas, examine data in developing a response, and then use the ABCs to guide how they responded.

In the process, Gordon discovered a lot about his territory and employees. He saw clearly where good management was already in place and where it wasn't. He stayed in touch with the good managers to show his support.

He went out of his way to talk candidly with those who were not measuring up, letting them know what he needed to see from them, providing direction, and helping them learn skills they needed.

By the end of Gordon's second or third field visit, word was out across his region: "Trafton really does expect us to change how we're doing our work. He's not going through the motions—this is for real. He wants every workplace to be a great place to work, and he expects every one of us to do our part. Standing on the sidelines is not an option."

Gordon Trafton made his sponsorship highly visible, a hallmark of leadership.

Example 2: Sponsoring a Safety-First Culture

Another executive, Keith Creel, took a different avenue to demonstrate his sponsorship. He chose to make safety the vehicle for bringing behavior-based culture change to his workforce.

Keith was the newly appointed SVP of CN's Eastern Canada Region, which spans operations from east of Winnipeg to Nova Scotia, with major rail yards in Toronto and Montreal.

In his region, Keith initially focused on changing the culture through creating an even safer work environment. He recognized positive leaders for their safety performance and then broadened their impact into other areas. He engaged his workforce by demonstrating his personal commitment to their safety and then invited their engagement in other areas. Safety was Keith's way of saying, "I'm sponsoring this change—are you with me?"

> How can we ask people to help us on asset utilization, cost management, customer satisfaction, reliability, or any of two dozen other key areas of improvement, if we don't provide a safe work environment and surround them with leaders and colleagues

who are 100 percent dedicated to their safe return home every night?

High performance starts with safety.

Keith used an existing venue to display his sponsorship of culture change: conference calls with key leaders across the region to review operations and issues.

Before Keith's tenure, these meetings had been highly irregular and poorly run. But under Keith, they became weekly—and sacred. He required his leadership team to be on the call, and be prepared. He expanded the calls to focus on leadership behavior and culture, and why both were urgently needed to address safety. His passion was evident from the very first call.

These calls became Keith's weekly opportunity to improve his region's DCOM® performance—at first on safety, and then for every area in his region. The following sections describe how he used DCOM®.

Improving the D (Direction)

Providing Direction just once is never enough. Keith repeated *what* he wanted to do and *why* until everyone got it.

To reinforce this, he used questions. He began every call by asking about each area's safety data, which showed that he was serious. People increasingly anticipated his questions, which meant they were increasingly clear on his Direction.

These calls also let Keith assess how well his leaders were aligned on Direction. He listened for two things:

1. How accurate were their answers? Could his people articulate the whys and whats?
2. Did they hesitate when answering? If someone had to think about their response, Keith's ABC training and coaching told him they were not yet *fluent.* But if they responded almost instantly, he knew they were getting the message in their soul, and his confidence grew that his team was solid on Direction.

Improving the C (Competence)

The weekly calls became teaching opportunities to ensure that everyone's Competence was up to the tasks they faced, whether managing for safety or for improved on-time train performance. As he delved into the root causes of a problem, Keith would listen to the skills and knowledge his people brought to the issue.

If he spotted a skill gap, Keith plugged it then and there. Gaps often were in technical railroad skills. But just as often, he would hear gaps in people skills, organizational skills, or leadership skills—especially in creating a safe workplace. These were all fair game for his teaching.

To move his region toward full engagement, Keith involved everyone. He did so by soliciting ideas on solving a problem and seeking the experience of team members who had faced similar issues. In this manner, Keith elevated everyone's Competence.

Improving the O (Opportunity)

It's up to leaders to provide employees the Opportunity to achieve their goals. Opportunity means providing funding, the right working environment, training, tools, and encouragement. But an especially important part of Opportunity is removing barriers, and for the barrier removal to cascade all the way to the front line.

Keith discovered barriers through direct questioning and astute listening:

- What must I—or we—do to get this done? What barriers need to get removed?
- How are you discovering what your team needs for success? Have you asked them? What did they say? What are you doing?

Keith listened carefully to deduce root causes. If he heard issues of process, staffing, resources, tools, technology, or a lack of information, he knew he had an Opportunity issue to address.

Keith is expert at shaping his team's behavior. During the earlier team calls, he carefully showed how he started with the symptom and then connected the dots step-by-step as he moved from symptom to the underlying root cause.

Then Keith shaped his team so they learned to connect the dots themselves, and he would ask them to identify the underlying Opportunity root cause. As the team learned to recognize symptoms, they would switch to identifying the root cause. Keith was teaching them to spot and solve Opportunity issues.

Keith washed away as much mud as he could. By removing the barriers, he visibly demonstrated that he was sponsoring the culture change in Eastern Canada. He also set the example for his team to follow in removing barriers themselves.

Improving the M (Motivation)

Even with all of this, Keith discovered that his region was not providing consistent consequences to ensure value-adding behavior. To his chagrin, leaders were not motivating the team as he had expected.

His ABC training enabled him to see some demotivating situations: Behaviors that undercut safety were being reinforced, while safe behaviors were getting punished. He tells this story:

> Before a CN railcar leaves our train yards, inspectors check it for safety problems. They look for ladders with jagged edges that could cut someone, a chain that could trip someone, something loose—anything. But to inspect a train with 100-plus railcars that stretches three-fourths of a mile, and inspect it on both sides, and do it thoroughly, takes a while.
>
> When our people did their job carefully—especially if they found a problem that required time to document and enter in our repair system—they frequently suffered some negative consequence when they returned to the inspection shop.
>
> Sometimes it was blatant: The boss would blow up in their faces. Other times it was subtle: The boss would make a sarcastic comment or roll his eyes at how long they'd taken to do the inspection.
>
> Positive leaders who were trying to do the right thing received exactly the wrong consequences. We had to stop this. So we worked on reinforcing the right behaviors and discouraging the wrong ones to improve our M—Motivation.

Keith knew that one solution to this was to enforce routine safety audits and reviews with employees. But he noticed that something wasn't right. Plenty of safety tests were reported (a safety test is a surprise inspection to make sure railroad crews are following safety rules). Yet Keith saw people taking risky shortcuts and not being held to safety standards.

He decided to talk directly with employees, and met one leaving his shift.

> "Hi, Bob. I see you had three safety tests last month."
>
> "Uh . . . safety tests?"
>
> "Yeah, your monthly safety tests. You passed them all. Has your supervisor Joe talked with you about them?"
>
> "Uh . . . no. You say he does them every month?"
>
> "Of course. Joe has to conduct at least three each month— and tell you how you did."
>
> "Oh."
>
> "That feedback helps you work safer. So I'll ask Joe to conduct another safety test for you next week—and give you the results. If you don't get his feedback by Friday, ask him for it."
>
> "Okay."
>
> "Bob, listen—the whole point is I want you to go home to Kate and the kids every night in the same shape you arrived in the morning, safe and sound."

Keith used his safety focus and team calls to display his sponsorship for the new culture. He modeled using the ABC tools, encouraged positive leaders, and challenged negative leaders to either get on board or get out.

He also got his people to work with their direct reports in the same way he worked with them. He constantly asked how they were engaging others—while he engaged them.

Example 3: Personally Walking the Talk

Claude Mongeau is CN's Chief Financial Officer and a powerful force in the company. A former Bain & Company consultant, he was named one of Canada's "Top 40 Under 40" (1997) and Canada's "CFO of the Year" (2005).

Like Hunter, Claude is part of that 15 percent of managers who intuitively understand how to bring out the best in people. He is a natural at tapping people's Discretionary Performance^{SM}.

But being natural at something often means that you can't articulate to others how you accomplish what you do. Your explanation is, "I don't know—I just do it!"

The ABCs helped Claude understand *why* he got the results from people that he did, and helped him realize that he needed to *visibly sponsor* the broader culture change initiative within Finance.

Visibly Demonstrating His Values

To make it real, Claude devised several ways to demonstrate the values he wanted in CN. One was learning. A lifelong reader and learner, Claude believes that all employees, especially those in staff jobs, need to fully understand the railroad business.

He decided that a good demonstration of how he values continuous learning would be to become certified as a railroad conductor. This is not the typical certification that an MBA/finance/major-league consultant would seek! It was time to break the mold.

The Real World of the Conductor

People commonly think of the conductor of a train as the person shouting "All aboard!" as the train pulls out of the station. But that's on a passenger train.

On a freight train, the conductor manages the train, which includes these duties:

- Obtain cargo loading/unloading information.
- Review the dispatcher's instructions.
- Maintain mobile communication with engineers, dispatchers, and conductors of other trains.
- Report mechanical difficulties and arrange for repairs.
- Arrange route changes when necessary.

By getting out of his office, into the rail yards, and learning this craft, Claude signaled to everyone in his financial organization that they needed to remember who they serve. He also signaled a reminder that the ultimate job is getting customers' cargo delivered on time.

He broke down hierarchy by being out in the yard wearing overalls, safety vest, and hard hat. He worked the radios, checked brakes, and inspected cars.

Employees discovered their CFO's down-to-earth nature. Word spread from yard to yard that management was taking this "new culture stuff" seriously. Here was CN's CFO, working side-by-side with unionized employees and eating lunch in the break room.

And he obviously was not putting on a one-day show. By working through all the requirements to become a certified conductor, Claude demonstrated that he was there to learn, however long it took.

It didn't stop there. Today, Claude is working to earn his Railroad MBA (Chapter 25). He is the most senior person in CN to do this. It is further testimony that CN's culture is changing, that railroading is all about operations, and that even the most senior staff need to understand this.

Sponsoring the ABC Workshops and Toolkit

Back inside his Finance unit, Claude visibly displayed his support in other ways. He started applying what he had learned from the ABCs:

- He altered how he ran staff meetings to encourage greater participation and openness.
- He pinpointed specific behaviors that he valued so his staff knew exactly what they had done to earn recognition.
- He shifted his personal style from "listen, then respond" to "inquire, then listen, then respond."

Claude used these means to visibly demonstrate his support and sponsorship for our culture change, and then effectively cascaded this sponsorship down through his organization. He sponsored the ABC workshops in all of his units and made sure the ABC Toolkit was used.

In Claude's already top-tier Finance unit, the improvements in results were clear. He made sure that everyone in his organization knew about the improvements in order to reinforce them.

Serge Pharand, Vice President and Corporate Controller, even started a feedback newsletter. In it, he shared a success story relating to integration activities:

> Our major achievement was the seamless integration of the GLT [Great Lakes Transportation] and BC Rail [British Columbia Rail] activities in our different functions. Even with many of our resources dedicated to this project, we were able to consistently maintain high-quality work in our day-to-day operations.

Applying the ABCs and making them work was a key factor in this achievement.

Cumulative billings to the end of November were 48 percent higher than for the same period last year. . . .

Similarly, collections have increased 52 percent. . . .

Claude had successfully embedded change deep in the Finance unit.

PART VI

ASSESSING SWITCHPOINTS' IMPACT

Once we had expanded the cultural change across the organization, we needed to assess our progress—were we on the right track? Assessing progress was critical to ensuring that we had made the right decisions at the key switchpoints. It also allowed us to demonstrate the value of the changes we were asking the organization to make.

18

Applying the ABCs:
Dressed & Ready

During the pilots, we discovered an old-culture behavior that was costing the company a lot of productivity and affecting everyone by the cultural tone it set. When we rolled out the ABCs more broadly, it became the first issue to be tackled.

It's a perfect example of how a little bit of time lost by everyone, every day, adds up to a great big cost. It could happen in any company. The difference was that CN fixed it.

Guess I'll Have Another Coffee . . .

On a typical day, employees would show up at the 7:30 A.M. start time, grab coffee, change into their work clothes, and wait for their supervisor to hand out daily assignments.

When the supervisors arrived, they developed the daily assignments, and then waited until everyone was assembled before posting them.

Once assignments were posted, employees returned to their lockers to get the safety equipment needed for their work that day, maybe grab another coffee, and then finally head out to work.

Can you hear the time clocks ticking away for everyone through all of this? And productivity slipping down the drain?

This process took employees 25 to 45 minutes every morning. With a crew of 20 people, *8 to 15 hours* were lost before the day's work had even started! And that was just one crew, at one rail yard, on one day. This was happening in several rail yards every day. Do the math and it was adding up to big dollars in unproductive labor and lost opportunity.

Not only that, it was an insult to the Five Guiding Principles. Trains were leaving late, affecting Service. Assets (locomotives, rail cars) were sitting or not being moved quickly. As a result, Costs were higher than necessary. CN's employees were not being led in a winning-team fashion.

Another Switchpoint

It was almost embarrassing to admit that CN had a problem like this. It was time to spike another switch.

Leaders started a new set of behavior and results expectations, called *Dressed & Ready*. Supervisors were to prepare assignments before they left work the previous day, posting them so that, when employees walked in for their next shift, they saw immediately what equipment they would need. This change meant that employees were able to go to their lockers only once and get everything they needed for the work day.

Start time was changed from "on-site by 7:30 A.M." to "in the common room, wearing appropriate equipment, and ready to go at 7:30 A.M." In other words: be Dressed & Ready for work.

Sound easy? Of course not. Like all bad habits, the old ingrained behavior was difficult to alter. As an organization, there were decades of comfortable old routines in place that both employees and managers didn't want to let go.

Put yourself in their position: You have a morning routine, driving to work over your normal route, listening to your favorite news or music, coffee at the same time, and so on. CN's employees had their morning routines. Supervisors were accustomed to the casual environment. They were afraid of the consequences for making waves.

The Science behind the Change

It's interesting to look at the ABCs to see how we changed the behavior of employees so they were Dressed & Ready for work. Remember, before Dressed & Ready, it was like this:

- *Antecedent:* Everyone knew the start time was 7:30 A.M.
- *Behavior:* People arrived at work by 7:15 A.M. and then got ready for their jobs by 8:15 A.M.
- *Consequences:* Everyone had time to socialize and have another coffee before starting to work. (This positive consequence drove people to maintain their late start to work.)

Clearly, this behavior had to change. Implementing the new Dressed & Ready behaviors required *changing the consequences to encourage the new behavior of being Dressed & Ready at start time, and to discourage the old behavior.*

In tackling Dressed & Ready, we drew on our positive leaders and positive followers and strengthened their influence relative to the negative leaders and negative followers. These positive leaders and followers had always wanted to put in a fair day's work for a fair day's wage. They didn't like starting late. But as long as management seemed unconcerned about this lax behavior, why should they speak out? Experience told them that they would only be hassled by the negative leaders and followers—a negative consequence.

The solution was to create new antecedents and consequences to drive the behavior change from starting work late to beginning on time.

New Antecedents to Trigger "Dressed & Ready" Behavior

The new antecedents set the stage for the new behavior.

- Employee meetings were held to point out the amount of time being lost each year across all of CN as a result of starting late (not being dressed and ready).
- Many of the employees were shareholders, so they were asked how they felt about their company losing this much productivity.
- Employees began talking about what they could do with this extra time to advance our Five Guiding Principles—in particular, working more safely, but also improving asset utilization, service (customer satisfaction), and cost management.
- These discussions gave positive leaders the opportunity to speak out. They also laid the groundwork for various work teams to set their own goals: "100 percent of us will be *Dressed & Ready*

by 7:30." As word spread of what these units did, others picked up the same goal—100 percent Dressed & Ready by 7:30.

- Management helped spread the word, of course—and then went through the organization reinforcing the position of the positive leaders and positive followers by letting everyone know that they were going to begin enforcing the existing policy.

New Consequences to Reinforce "Dressed & Ready" Behavior

Previously, supervisors did nothing to reinforce employees' behavior of being Dressed & Ready to begin work by 7:30 A.M. Now their ABC training and coaching taught them to provide positive consequences for this new behavior:

- Supervisors started in the locker rooms prior to 7:30. They made eye contact with each person who showed up on time and gave a slight and silent nod, or shook a hand, or said "Thanks"—whatever worked best with each employee.
- For some employees, visibly shaking hands with a supervisor could mean grief out in the train yard. In such cases, supervisors worked with their coach to plan the best way to reinforce specific individuals. Often they would seek out those employees later in the day, when they were working alone, to thank them privately. Or they would radio the person.
- As entire shifts showed up Dressed & Ready (the 100 percent that some teams had committed to), supervisors shifted from reinforcing individuals to thanking the whole team.
- After four or five consecutive days of 100 percent Dressed & Ready, supervisors were coached to do something special. Many told their teams, "Hey—this is the fifth day in a row 100 percent of you have been *Dressed & Ready* on time—this is terrific! So . . . you all have been after me to get a new microwave for the break area. I've got $250—who would like to go buy a microwave?"

These positive consequences began to gain momentum. More and more teams started showing up 100 percent Dressed & Ready. Supervisors, attuned to the power of spreading the good word, intentionally swapped stories with their crews about how "I bragged on our team to (another manager or a CN higher-up) that we've gone 15 weeks with 100 percent *Dressed & Ready* every day!"

New Consequences to Extinguish Starting-Late Behavior

Before, supervisors let the undesired behavior of starting late slip by without consequences. Now, their ABC education and coaching taught them that by doing nothing about it, they were actually reinforcing the behavior of starting late.

Supervisors knew they had to provide negative consequences for late starts—and through the coaching they'd received, they knew how to do it with precision and skill:

- In most cases, the first time an employee started late, he was talked to by his supervisor.
- The second time, the employee was more formally reprimanded.
- The third time, the employee was suspended for the day without pay—exactly the remedy allowed for in CN's labor agreements, but a remedy that had been used only sporadically and inconsistently in the past.

How Senior Leaders Helped

Senior leaders knew they had to do their part, too:

- When visiting a site, they knew in advance the site's latest Dressed & Ready data and would mention it at every stop. If a local supervisor requested, they'd praise Dressed & Ready results in an e-mail posting in a break area.
- Senior leaders also knew their first-line supervisors needed continuing support in their struggle with negative leaders. They backed up the supervisors as they moved through CN's progressive discipline process. Indeed, some employees never really got it and eventually had to be let go. As word of this consequence spread, it further convinced fence-sitters that leaders meant it about everyone showing up Dressed & Ready by 7:30. They started hopping off the fence, and their teams started receiving positive consequences from their supervisors.

Of Course There Was Resistance!

When the culture change began, you can imagine the backlash. People not only were accustomed to the old culture—they had no reason to even question their practices. For those who had grown up in the old culture, the new demands seemed unreasonable, as if the company were asking too much.

Union and management both protested Dressed & Ready. Many managers struggled with the new rules. They weren't comfortable ordering employees to change the way they worked. But we proceeded one switchpoint at a time, spiking each switch as we passed through it, guiding CN through a culture change that would pay great dividends to all.

With changes like Dressed & Ready, many thought it was all about making employees do things differently. But that wasn't so. The toughest part was convincing managers of the need to change, and then getting them to hold firm. It was important that all of them agreed and were consistent in enforcing Dressed & Ready.

Many had never been asked to hold people accountable for performance, even with something basic like showing up for work on time. Some managers feared retaliation.

"I Can't Ask My Friends to Do That!"

Most of our supervisors had come up through the union ranks. They knew what it was like to do the assignments they handed out, and how tough some days could be. They had become so entrenched in the old culture that some saw themselves as friends, not leaders.

When you've been a co-worker and friend, it's hard to become the one in charge, especially when no one tells you how to act in your role. People stay with what they know, and supervisors knew how to go along to get along. This behavior paid off in the past, at least in keeping peace between managers and employees, and they saw no reason to change it.

As Q4 Leadership^{SM} spread, some people were able to make the change. However, the harsh reality is that some Q2 leaders could not change their stripes and become effective Q4 leaders.

The hardest cases were the nice people. Les Dakens tells this story:

> Shortly after Dressed & Ready was rolled out, I was with Hunter and others at a business plan rollout in one of CN's key cities.

During a break, we dropped in on an ABC training session being conducted in the same facility. It was a great opportunity to get some face-to-face feedback and show support for the ABC process.

These visits had always been enjoyable. But this day was different.

At one of the tables, a long-service supervisor spoke to the table and the senior leader who had just arrived.

"I know the ABCs are all good stuff, but there's no way I can ask my guys to do this."

"Do what?" someone asked.

"This come-on-time, be-ready-to-work, Dressed & Ready stuff. I can't ask my friends to do that!"

We were shocked. Here was a leader who was saying that he couldn't ask people to do the minimum on their jobs, because he viewed them as friends! The discussion continued later outside the meeting room, yet no reasoning would move him from his position. We had to admire his honesty. Many people would have shut up and spouted the corporate line.

Here was our challenge: What would we do with a long-service, honest, up-front, hardworking employee who couldn't do what we required of a leader? It was a test for us. Was our organization truly committed to doing what we must to ensure that we had Q4 leaders to move the culture?

The organization was watching. How were we going to treat good people who couldn't become Q4 leaders and drive the culture change? We had to act fast.

So we did what we felt was right, both for the company and the employee. We moved him—that very day—out of a people-leading position to a staff role that would use his tremendous knowledge and experience, but without managing people.

Over time, we found that this pattern repeated itself, and we had to migrate more good people into roles better suited to their personal characteristics.

Not every case worked out, though. One notable Q3 leader just couldn't make the transition and wouldn't have worked out in another role. Again, the organization was watching us. The great neutral majority was looking to see what we would do.

In this case, after many coaching sessions, the person had to leave CN. That we were willing to let someone go who could deliver results told many doubters that we were very serious.

The Rewards of "Dressed & Ready"

An unexpected plus emerged from spiking the switch on Dressed & Ready. Some employees had always arrived on time and put in their full day of work, despite what those around them did. They did so not because it was demanded, but because they knew it was right.

These people had been inadvertently punished for doing the right thing. They were earning the same pay as the person who came in late, took long breaks, and left early. Some had even been shunned in the past for their dedication.

Now they were becoming recognized as leaders and early adopters. This outcome was just what we needed to help keep the momentum. When people are rewarded positively—in this case with recognition and the chance for influence—their behavior gets reinforced. It also makes other people, who may have been hanging back and waiting to see what would happen before they changed their behavior, want to gain the same positive rewards.

Today, being Dressed & Ready is part of the fabric in CN's workforce. The surest test is when a work team tells every newcomer: "This is how we do it here. We are *Dressed & Ready* at 7:25 in our unit, so we're out the door at 7:30. You better not let us down!"

When this happens, you know you've successfully spiked a key switchpoint and changed the culture in a small way. This was a tough switchpoint for everyone. But we succeeded in taking this big leap in culture change—not to mention the substantial impact on business results.

19

Early Wins with the ABCs

As we rolled out the ABCs more broadly across the organization, we saw leaders take on new ideas and create change with their teams. This change took shape differently in different parts of the company, based on the needs of the business and leaders.

As we said, many roads lead to Rome. The leaders' stories shared here show just a few of the many roads we took, and how these leaders absorbed the training and created their own pathways to improvement. These are examples of early successes, each story describing how changes in behavior created improvements in one or more of the Five Guiding Principles.

Release the Brakes!

Service

Asset
Utilization

Cost
Control

Safety

Each railcar has a handbrake that can be set to prevent the car from rolling. This is necessary because at some locations railroad tracks have slight slopes. Unless the handbrakes are applied, a railcar can roll, becoming a runaway with the potential to injure someone.

Once a train is ready to leave the terminal, we must be certain that the handbrake has been released on every car in the train. This can mean checking well over 100 cars.

The simple failure to release a brake can cause an expensive, time-consuming incident:

- If the brake is not fully released, the wheel drags along the track and three things happen: Heat builds up, the wheel develops a flat spot, and we waste many gallons of fuel dragging that car instead of it rolling freely like it's supposed to.
- Once the brake is eventually released, with every turn of the wheel the flat spot hits the rail, doing so with a force many times greater than if the wheel were truly round. This extra force can actually shatter steel rails and cause a derailment.
- The heat buildup from a dragging wheel can ignite brush or trash that's accumulated along the right of way (one reason we spend millions each year maintaining our roadbeds).
- When an unreleased brake is discovered, we stop the train and the conductor walks to the offending car and releases the brake—which can delay the train (and any others coming behind it) up to 20 minutes.

In terms of our Five Guiding Principles, this simple behavior of not fully releasing every brake ends up affecting Asset Utilization, Cost, Service, and Safety. So every handbrake must be released.

Here is one leader's story of using the ABCs to solve the handbrake problem:

> Our yard in Fond du Lac, Wisconsin, had an unusually high number of handbrake problems. This was due primarily to the significant slope of the yard, which required setting a higher number of handbrakes on railcars to prevent runaways. But why were the brakes not always released properly?
>
> A team that included three departments (Transportation, Mechanical, Engineering) sought the root cause. They discovered that multiple employees had responsibility for releasing handbrakes. This led to someone occasionally assuming that someone else would release a brake. This was a setup for failure.
>
> So the team clarified who was expected to do this checking. We improved the situation from confusion across three departments to clarity.
>
> Another root cause was that employees would visually inspect the handbrake chain, and if it looked slack, they assumed the brake was off—but sometimes it wasn't.

So the team pinpointed a simple but critical behavior change: Instead of visually inspecting handbrake chains, employees had to physically tug on the chains to check tension. If a chain felt slack, they would be certain the brake was released. Employees were coached in this new behavior.

Before we used the ABC Toolkit to help change this process and behavior, Fond du Lac averaged three handbrake incidents per week. After the team's recommendations were implemented, incidents plummeted to 0.54 per week, an 82 percent reduction. Cost savings were substantial, eliminating thousands of dollars in repairs.

CN credits the ABCs for this improvement, because it encouraged the behaviors of cross-functional troubleshooting and cooperation among the three departments, and devised a robust behavioral solution. What once was a pass-the-blame situation now had clear direction, behaviors, and consequences.

Culture Change in the Michigan Division

Service   Asset Utilization   Cost Control   People

The ABCs help us clearly see our behaviors as process steps that link people to activities in support of our Five Guiding Principles. Now we're spotting unprofitable business and ways to do things better, faster, and cheaper.

We are now consistently using data. We are asking pinpointed questions to help us drill to root causes. We listen carefully instead of jumping to conclusions. Better listening has created valuable two-way feedback up, down, and sideways.

CLG consultant Marcia Corbett tells this story of working with Mike Cory and the leadership team in Michigan. Their attention to behavior improved performance in several areas:

> Our trip plans indicate the door-to-door time for each customer, which we measure, a practice that sharply differentiates CN from other railroads. Our goal for adhering to trip plans is 95 percent, and we have been running at that and

above, despite inclement weather and other factors beyond our control.

We're experiencing a breakthrough in communication with our unionized employees. In some areas, we've been tough about attendance and they've told us how we can help them. We are seeing an improvement without having to discipline people.

We've met with unionized employees at various terminals, and they brought the same data that we had. We've talked with our employees—those positive leaders Peter Edwards talks about—and they've told us how we can improve attendance.

She also cites examples of major culture change:

Supervisors have gone from just saying "hi" to working with employees to correct problems in support of our Five Guiding Principles. We're empowering them to work as a group and solve problems.

We're observing people who need help because they are doing new things. We leaders help by applying consequences, and we're starting to see the benefit.

One division started a weekly meeting that includes the departments of Engineering, Track Repair, Mechanical, and Transportation. By cutting across silos that historically have been really strong, they found numerous ways to reduce labor and out-of-service time for equipment.

At one site, a superintendent gathered about 20 employees to work together on improving their service offering. These people are now spreading it down to their reports.

Our new thinking helped an employee who works on the manpower planning report. For months he had received data without questioning it and plugged it into a formula. We included him in a study of the process. Now, on his own, he is reviewing the data and asking valuable questions to ensure that we are making the right decisions. He sees that he has a voice and knows that we'll listen.

The feedback has built confidence in people, opening them to learning more. We're no longer afraid to fix things that don't work. Supervisors are saying, "Hey, we can get data now and change this."

The ABCs Improve ETAs

Service

Asset
Utilization

Cost
Control

In our business, estimated time of arrival (ETA) drives the whole planning process.

Of our Five Guiding Principles, Service is the one that drives us to be on time, all the time. The behavior of every single employee affects being on time, but a heavy part of the responsibility lies with Railroad Traffic Control (RTC).

RTC employees manage train movement between locations. They work in a control room somewhat like an air traffic control center. It has computer screens that show the status of the trains in green (on time), yellow (5 to 59 minutes late), red (60 or more minutes late), pink (so far off schedule that we just park the train and reschedule it), or blue (more than 30 minutes early, which can be just as disruptive as being late).

RTC plans each train's trip by preparing an ETA. Thus, the ETA is the critical beginning data point for the complex process of getting a train from A to B on time. If you have an erroneous ETA forecast, it affects service, asset utilization, and cost. As one leader explained:

> We had plenty of poor ETA forecasts. During one three-day snapshot:
>
> - 82 percent of trains arrived on time, based on a 1-hour ETA (an ETA predicted 1 hour before the train arrived)
> - 75 percent of trains arrived on time, based on a 2-hour ETA
> - 70 percent of trains arrived on time, based on a 3-hour ETA
> - 39 percent of trains arrived on time, based on a 4-hour ETA
>
> This was not so good. The ETAs were way too erratic. Pardon the pun, but this was no way to run a railroad!
>
> We went to the RTC center. "It's mission-critical to get better ETAs. They drive your whole planning process," we told them. The key was to improve the process and get the behaviors needed for better forecasting to happen.

They put a new process in place and went to the forecasting people. They explained why it is important to forecast accurately and how the forecast is used, so the RTC people understood that it's not just an exercise of plugging numbers into a computer, and that their work has a very critical impact. They linked process improvement to behavior.

Improvement was dramatic:

- 93 percent of trains arrived on-time, based on a 1-hour ETA.
- 89 pe.rcent of trains arrived on-time, based on a 2-hour ETA.
- 85 percent of trains arrived on-time, based on a 3-hour ETA.
- 78 percent of trains arrived on-time, based on a 4-hour ETA.

This was accomplished by a group who had been through our ABC workshops, and they did it on their own. We created the metrics, but they accomplished most of the work on their own, setting the right expectations, coaching people, measuring performance, and working with those who were not doing as well as others.

The amazing part is that they did it almost overnight. Within a week, they had made substantial improvements. Now the RTC folks say they want to go even further. They're trying to look out eight hours ahead.

Want Better Meetings? Show Up on Time!

Service

People

"The field had long believed that all we did was have meetings," said Kim Simmonds of the IT department. "And that's true, but it's the nature of our work—we have to get people together to decide and plan things." The problem was the quality of the meetings, which did not run like clockwork.

So when 40 of our IT managers attended ABC training, they selected their first behavior to change: Employees were to arrive on time for meetings.

At first, some laughed at what appeared to be a silly choice. Others cynically said it was impossible. But the more they talked about it, the more senior leaders believed that this simple behavior change would improve meeting quality markedly. And the majority of employees felt that showing up at meetings on time was the least people could do to show respect for others' time.

They saw multiple benefits: Improve meeting effectiveness, streamline decision making, maximize people's productivity, and improve IT's image.

CLG consultant Brenda Chartrand tells what happened:

> The team's initial ABC analysis, using DCOM® to identify antecedents, revealed that no formal guidelines existed to help chairpersons plan and run effective meetings. Kim Simmonds researched this on the web and the team created its first "A" (antecedent): a "Guide to Conducting Effective Meetings."
>
> The guide contains basic guidelines on:
>
> - How to develop an agenda.
> - Clarifying the roles of chairperson and member.
> - Types of meetings (for example, update/status or decision making).
> - The 48-hour rule (conclude issues and decisions within 48 hours of the meeting—streamlining the process and not letting decisions drag on).
> - Criteria for well-organized meetings and signs of poorly organized meetings.
>
> The team also looked at the facilitation skills of the people leading meetings. They put together a tip sheet on running successful meetings. This later became an audit tool for tracking the key behavior—showing up on time for meetings.
>
> Under Kim's direction, IT created a web site for these antecedent documents, communicated the ABC plan to all directors and meeting chairpersons, and scheduled a go-live date.
>
> Initially, IT directors randomly spot-checked meetings and gave feedback to chairpersons. "Until the audit at one of their meetings, people thought this was a bad thing," Kim said. "But once it was done, they agreed the feedback helped them see how to run a better meeting."
>
> Kim then arranged for audit pads in all major meeting rooms. A volunteer at each meeting would tear off an audit sheet and Kim processed the data, posting audit charts in all meeting rooms.

Having a volunteer do a quick evaluation of the meeting took pressure off the meeting chairperson to track who was on time, was there an agenda, was it followed, and so on. The meeting chairperson gave feedback to attendees who did not arrive on time.

Individual on-time performance rose to over 80 percent, and the number of people coming late dropped sharply—all because of attention to the right critical behavior. It seems like a small thing, but think of the time and momentum lost when ten people are interrupted by one.

Small Things Matter

Service   Asset   Cost   People
                 Utilization   Control

Running a Precision Railroad is highly advantageous to the people who use our services. Our trip plans show our customers the precise plan for their shipments—where each of their rail cars will be and when it will arrive. CN's trip plan compliance is the best in the business. But as hard as we try, we still have occasional trip plan failures.

Clerical errors account only for a small percentage of these, but these small things matter when you're working hard to be the best in customer service (the number one Guiding Principle).

Suzanne Van Huis, a Senior Customer Service Manager, notes:

> We make a commitment to our customer for every rail car. Whether we receive the cars directly from the customer or they are handed off to us from another railroad, we make a time commitment to deliver.
>
> Whenever a railcar moves, it must be reported accurately in the computer, just like FedEx and UPS track their packages at every point. But if a clerical person or conductor makes a mistake in reporting a car location, a trip plan failure could result.

Suzanne's division studied everything that impacted trip plan compliance. They noted that Transportation Reporting Services, which tracks the location of customers' shipments, can input incorrect data in their rush of work. So we developed an ABC action plan with a results target of 100 percent reporting accuracy to eliminate clerical trip plan failures.

To achieve that accuracy, we had to minimize every opportunity for error. Suzanne continues:

> Our reps are always multitasking because they report on trains for several stations. Calls from different locations keep them busy and can lead to distraction.
>
> Our group identified five critical behaviors that reps always needed to perform. We called them the "Five Keys to Trip Plan Success":
>
> 1. Minimize distractions. Is your door closed? Do your calls roll into voice mail? Have you minimized other computer programs?
> 2. Scan the document. Is it legible? Are all fields completed? Is it signed? Are there questions?
> 3. Highlight as you go. Use yellow highlighter to highlight only work that you've completed.
> 4. Respond to all "not done" codes. Refer to the "Not Done Code & Response Chart."
> 5. Spot-check your work as time permits. Use the Trains files on the Customer Service drive to note exceptions.

These all seem very simple, even obvious. But in every workplace, the simple and obvious doesn't always happen, so we needed conscientious focus on those behaviors.

Our kickoff drew attention to the new program, and we gave each rep a laminated card showing the five key behaviors. Reps stuck this card to their computers to always have the list in front of them. Managers did visual spot-checks of the clerical staff, observing their use of the five key behaviors. In Transportation, the customer service team held work order training to show conductors how to properly fill out work orders.

When the service reps first heard of our action plan, they thought the 100 percent goal was unattainable. But as weeks went by without any failures, they became more enthusiastic and involved.

Suzanne concludes:

> We've had a few setbacks, and you can see them in the chart. Twice we had groups of 14 and 16 cars that hurt our statistics.

But both times a wrong date was keyed in and the service rep caught and corrected the error within minutes. They still counted as trip plan failures, but overall we've improved a lot.

Employees are seeing clearly that what they do affects the entire car cycle and its trip plan. It has given them the bigger picture of how their reporting affects the railroad.

Curing Technophobia

Service

Asset
Utilization

Cost
Control

Safety

People

When the U.S. Federal Railroad Administration mandated that we had to electronically record all of our signal testing, Manager of Signals John Rath saw trouble brewing:

My team had recorded signal information using paper and pencil from the dawn of time, and now they were faced with these new electronic handheld devices.

The new Signal Equipment Tracking system (SETs) devices gave us the ability to analyze enormous amounts of data quickly and efficiently. But folks here initially thought the new system seemed too complicated and meant unnecessary additional work.

As I came to understand the technology, I saw the advantages of the SETs handhelds:

1. They allow better management of our parts inventory through immediate updates and greater accuracy.
2. They help us surpass federal requirements for documentation.
3. They put all the information that Signal Supervisors gather into a common repository so anyone can see the big picture.

Our zone performs more than 60,000 signal tests each month. Limited manpower added to the challenge for already-stretched employees who were asked to increase testing to the new standards—a 25 percent increase in their work volume. Some employees feared that the computer would lose their data, which in fact actually happened once.

To accomplish this difficult change, we developed an ABC action plan to reinforce the desired new behavior: *All employees use SETs device to record tests.* We set a goal of 100 percent compliance by a deadline date.

I communicated the plan in a letter to employees. I laid out milestones I expected the group to hit—increasing monthly goals of 10 percent, 25 percent, 50 percent, 75 percent, and finally 100 percent of testing done with SETs.

The plan included having computer-proficient employees mentor those who were less technology-savvy. I also supported the launch with color posters and regular reminders that reinforced the 100 percent goal.

Whenever the entire group reached an interim goal, I distributed motivational messages on cups, light pens, and lanyards.

Throughout the process, I regularly encouraged my supervisors to reinforce the new behavior with positive feedback. Supervisors were responsible for training and coaching employees.

By closely monitoring the leading behavioral indicators, I observed that one group was behind schedule. I learned that this group's manager was not enforcing the new requirement. This behavior became an opportunity for me to refocus that manager on giving Direction (the D in DCOM®) and why it was important.

Our Signal Team hit their compliance target of 100 percent. But this is an ongoing project. We are still applying the ABCs as we continue to use SETs devices to record our tests.

The preceding stories were taken straight from the leaders and consultants who lived them. While each leader's path was different, each utilized the ABC tools to identify and drive behavior changes that would impact one or more of the Five Guiding Principles. They were early indications of the change we could create if we rallied the organization toward a new culture.

20

Demonstrating Q4 Leadership℠ Through the ABCs

Several leaders shared stories with us of early wins that they attribute to their use of the ABCs in their development of Q4 Leadership℠ skills. Three of those stories are shared below.

"More Work? Are You Nuts?!"

In the city of Edmonton, amidst Alberta's fertile prairieland, lies one of our two main rail yards in western Canada. Walker Yard bustles with 3,000 railcars daily. Its maintenance shop was suddenly tasked with a dramatic workload increase. This leader tells how he used Q4 Leadership℠ to meet the challenge and create exceptional results.

> Atop our normal workload came this special order: Modify 200 ventilated railcars, the type we use to haul paper products. We were to finish a dozen per week, which would add about 400 man-hours to our load. This was budgeted capital work for completion by year's end.
>
> After a few months, we were $700,000 over budget, with not one car completed. "We're never going to make it," supervisors complained. "We lack manpower, our workload's still high, and we're still recovering from the strike."
>
> In earlier times, Q3 leadership might have gotten hard-nosed and demanded overtime. But this was a time for Q4 leadership,

a time to listen and work together. I asked shop employees for their ideas on how to get the work done. Together, we agreed:

- To refine our process flow, make sure it was followed, and reconfigure the workshop to fit the new flow.
- To dedicate people to the extra work, plus shift some mechanics from other work to this task.
- To communicate the urgency and goal to all.

Everyone generated ideas, and work began to move. Q4 Leadership^{SM} was working.

But then *another* budgeted task appeared: Replace wheel assemblies on our grain cars—a high priority, with the grain harvest season barreling toward us—and complete the first 25 by year's end.

"*More work?* Are you nuts?!" declared one supervisor. It was Q4 time again. I said, "Get everyone together and look at our process again. What can we do better?" The deeper we drilled, the more we found:

- Instead of moving people and jobs from one maintenance track to another, as we had always done, we dedicated each track so the same work was always done there, and dedicated people to each track. This made work consistent day-to-day, plus people could see their progress and build ownership.
- We reassigned people based on their best talents and skills.
- We moved the routine daily repairs out of the shop and into the open rail yard, freeing the shop for the special work.

Our year-end success: All 200 ventilated cars were completed, plus three times our target on the grain cars. We even maintained our low percentage of out-of-service railcars. (That target was to have less than 1.5 percent out for repair. A 0.5 percent change in this number roughly equals 2,500 railcars across CN.)

Halfway through the following year, Q4 Leadership^{SM} proved itself again: We completed double our grain car target and lowered the percentage of out-of-service cars by nearly half.

This work hit all of our Five Guiding Principles. For Assets, Service, and Cost, we improved railcars and their availability at lower cost. For Safety, we saw a 58 percent safety improvement. And it was only with our people's commitment that the goals were met and exceeded.

People were skeptical of our new Q4 Leadership^{SM} style at first. But now some negative leaders have turned around, and there is much less confrontation. Union grievances dropped promptly—we now discuss issues before they even get written down.

We achieved a revolution at Walker Yard in only six months.

What we learned from this achievement:

- Changing our leadership style to Q4 was critical to unlocking employees' Discretionary Performance^{SM} (they never would have worked so well under Q3 leadership).
- Q4 Leadership^{SM} wasn't obvious and had to be coached (so we did some coaching).
- Everyone, from negative leader to positive leader, was watching to see if we would stick with it and make Q4 Leadership^{SM} work (we did).

This story demonstrates the lift that leaders can cause when they change their leadership style to really engage their teams. It wasn't only the employees who had to adjust to the culture change—so did the leaders, learning to lead the Q4 way.

Improving Reliability: Getting KIST

Here is a second example of Q4 Leadership^{SM} in action. A CN regional engineer tells this story of an inspection program to keep employees productive and to improve track safety:

When our maintenance crews do repairs on a section of track, they often must wait for approaching trains to pass before they can start working safely. Sometimes their wait is long as a train approaches from 20 or 30 miles away. It always frustrated me that we would have sizable crews sitting idle for so long.

Then I had an idea. To recover this lost time, I asked my managers to find a way to turn all of our maintenance workers into basic track inspectors. My purpose was not to replace our official track inspectors. The idea was to augment the number of inspections done while also giving maintenance employees productive work as they awaited the all clear that it was safe to begin work.

My managers immediately came up with a detailed spreadsheet with 34 procedures for maintenance employees to follow! While I appreciated their zeal, I also saw that they were trying to turn maintenance employees into full-fledged track inspectors. This complicated things too much.

I reminded them of the old KISS acronym—Keep It Simple, Stupid—and asked them to work with Steve Quesnelle, our CLG consultant. The team returned in a week and, with their dry engineering wit, said they had reengineered KISS into KIST: Kick, Inspect, Sweep, Touch.

These were four simple behaviors that maintenance employees could conduct, with a simple acronym to help them remember: *Kick* the bolts that hold rails together to ensure they are tight. *Inspect* switchpoints for debris like rocks, wood, or sand that could interfere with switch operation. *Sweep* debris from the switchpoints if necessary. *Touch* the electrical bond wires that connect rails together to ensure they are welded firmly.

Supervisors held one-on-one meetings with maintenance employees to explain what to look for, and gave them colorful job aids that outlined the KIST behaviors and used photographs to help them recognize problem areas.

Employees used a daily KIST tracking form to capture their activities, any anomalies they found, and what was done about them. If it was a serious problem, they contacted the track supervisor.

Supervisors tallied data at the end of each week, and the leadership team summarized findings and determined root causes. Within two months, employees completed over 2,000 additional inspections.

All employees reported finding many items. Supervisors gave them positive feedback and used CNAP Cards (the CN Appreciation Program) to reward them for exceptional effort.

Employees took this on diligently and enthusiastically and now regard it as their duty to stop and look for trouble. Some even travel up and down the track more often, just to kick, inspect, sweep, and touch—a perfect example of Discretionary Performance^{SM}.

Q4 Leadership^{SM} again showed its value: clear expectations, shared measurement, and constant, consistent feedback.

Understanding Q4 Leadership℠— by Knowing What It Is Not

Gordon Trafton is Senior Vice President for the railway's Southern Region, encompassing the United States and portions of Canada. Gordon is a quiet, unassuming, but powerful advocate of Q4 Leadership℠.

He points out that a good way to understand Q4 Leadership℠ is to take a reverse view and look at what it is *not*. The following list outlines his view.

- *Q4 Leadership℠ is not about being nice—it is about leading to get results.* Q4 Leadership℠ defines several things: the exact results we seek, what behaviors will get those results, and the specific consequences needed to make those behaviors happen.

    This means that Q4 leaders must spend more time with their employees, getting out in the office or plant or shop where the work is done, always listening and inviting conversation and never shutting it down. (Being nice, by the way, just comes naturally as part of this better contact between leaders and employees!)

- *Q4 Leadership℠ is not about too many back pats, which can actually makes things worse.* Behavioral scientists know that the surest way to promote Discretionary Performance℠ is through encouragement and positive feedback. Unfortunately, some leaders leap to faulty conclusions. Because encouragement is such a powerful tool, some assume that it's the only one. But Q4 leaders still use discouragement—selectively and knowingly.

    The difference is that Q3 leaders are negative far more often, making things personal instead of keeping them about business. That's destructive and wins only short-term results. The Q4 leader uses consequences carefully, with clear understanding of their impact.

- *Q4 Leadership℠ is not about manipulating people to squeeze more work out of them.* It *is* about making your expectations clear, being precise about how people's performance will be measured, and giving people plenty of feedback and coaching.

    Before you demand performance from people, set them up for success. Make sure they're clear on the goal. Confirm that they have the right training, skills, and experience.

Give them resources and remove barriers. Make sure they're motivated to deliver what's expected.

If an employee has a performance gap, coach him to close it. Spend time listening. Learn when to coach rather than teach. Above all, model the behaviors you expect from others.

To sum up, Q4 Leadership^{SM} is about:

- Making your expectations clear, objectively assessing performance using well-understood measures, and always giving feedback and coaching—not to criticize, but to help employees improve.
- Encouraging every employee with tailored consequences, spending as much time listening as talking, and helping struggling employees get it right.
- Modeling the behavior you ask of others, and walking the talk yourself.

Spreading Q4 Leadership^{SM} across the company created a common vocabulary for culture change. This was especially important because of CN's multiple countries, languages, and cultures.

21

Life or Death Leadership

In any heavy industry, safety is serious business. But on the railroad, it's dead serious.

In 2007, the U.S. Federal Railroad Administration reported 2,330 accidents on railways and in rail yards (this excludes accidents involving the public at highway rail crossings and trespassing). Of these, there were 175 collisions, 1,696 derailments, and eight fatalities. Primary causes were human factors (about 38 percent), track defects (about 35 percent), and equipment defects (about 12 percent). About half of all accidents occurred in rail yards.

Most safety rules in place today are the result of lessons learned the hard way over many decades of railroading. At CN, if we are passionate about our other four Guiding Principles, we are fanatical about the one for Safety. It's the number one thing that keeps us up at night, because many of us have felt the impact of close calls, either personally or through witnessing those of co-workers.

A Grim Tale

Every major industry has horror stories about safety. One of ours comes from a first-line manager at one of our major terminals. It illustrates why we place so much emphasis on safety.

> After one ABC session, a few managers were gathered, talking about their experiences, when one spoke in a quiet, unsteady voice. He talked about being a first-line manager at one of our major terminals one day when they were all hustling to get a

train out. One of his people, a great young man, thought he saw something hanging on the other side of the train. The train had not coupled up yet, so the young man decided to dart through between the uncoupled cars.

His heart was in the right place—he wanted to keep things moving—but the moment he got between the cars, the train pushed back and the two segments coupled on him, catching him right through the middle. Alarms were sounded and the train was stopped and there he was, coupled through the middle and alive.

A doctor was sent for. He came quickly, examined the young man, and said that when the train was uncoupled, the young man would essentially break in two and die. If it was left coupled, he would also die, it would just take longer.

Immediately, the supervisor got into the company truck and, with tears streaming down his face, drove to the employee's home, knocked on the door, and told the young man's wife that she had to come. Her husband was dying and there was little time left.

She gathered up her children to take them to see their father for the last time. When they arrived, a sheet had been placed around him so that only his upper body could be seen. The next moments were between a man and his wife and a father and his children. When their brief time was over, the children were led away, and the young man's wife stayed with him until he died, the cars were uncoupled, and his body was removed.

This is a very graphic and painful story, but when you think about it, it could have been prevented. Every day, employees make decisions about how to do the right thing. As leaders, peers, and friends, we have an obligation to help them see that even a small bending of the rules can be catastrophic.

A behavior that ignores the rules can have a huge impact, not just on one person, but on an ever-widening circle of people. This is why we work hard to build a safety culture at CN.

Safety and Culture Change

Safety was and is very much a part of our culture change. Safety is one of our Five Guiding Principles, and the foundation of our success. We could not progress as a company if we failed to keep employees healthy and injury-free.

The key to making our improved safety culture is to *constantly reinforce safety behaviors*. As you know by now, we do that by managing *consequences*.

Standards don't start to slip on a date circled on a calendar. No memo is issued. It happens a little every day, by

- Overlooking an unsafe action.
- Not correcting someone's risky action.
- Failing to raise the issue with a co-worker who is acting unsafely.

To succeed in changing the culture, we couldn't let safety slip. If leaders couldn't discuss something as important and personal as safety with employees, or hold them accountable for acting safely, then there was no point in trying to change anything else.

Developing Safety Programs

Most industrial safety programs feature the well-known safety pyramid. As shown in Figure 21.1, for every fatal accident, there is an average of 30 lost work days, 300 recordable injuries, 3,000 near-misses, and 300,000 risky behaviors.

The point of the safety pyramid is to demonstrate that each level of the pyramid builds upon the level below it. To reduce fatalities, start by reducing at-risk behaviors. Change the culture to get rid of all risky behaviors, and the injuries will plummet toward zero. That's exactly the point of a safety culture.

We tackled at-risk behaviors by creating great awareness of our safety rules. We developed shift huddles, safety walkabouts, and "SaFE^{SM}" observations.

Shift Huddles

At the beginning of every shift, team leads met with their teams to review the work ahead of them. In the brief huddle, they asked "What could hurt us today?" They ensured that everyone was equipped and ready to complete their assigned duties.

Safety Walkabouts

A group of leaders regularly walks the rail yard, looking for employees who are engaging in safe behaviors and discussing with them

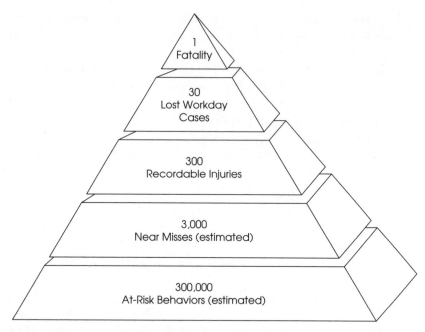

Figure 21.1   The Safety Pyramid
Source: CLG.

opportunities to make the yard safer yet. Doing these walkabouts helps the leadership team calibrate what they agree to be safe. It also enables open, honest discussions with employees about rules, yard conditions, and safe behaviors.

HR Manager Terry Gallagher recounts the value of safety walkabouts and the culture change they helped create:

> I love safety walkabouts. They get everyone talking. Typically, a walkabout includes me with a supervisor or two. We walk about the rail yard and review employee safety performance. We look for people following procedures so we can praise them, and people who aren't—*not to catch them, but to coach them.*
>
> We also talk about the ABCs, how we work and why, why we are there, and then invite employees to talk about concerns or ideas they have to make their jobs safer. We're there to coach—and to listen.
>
> At first, people would spot us and say, "Uh-oh, the white hats are coming," referring to the white safety hats worn by management. That was code for "Everyone get to work, or

you'll get chewed out." They'd be working away, wouldn't even acknowledge us, and had nothing to say if we asked. It was punishing for them and us. But today, they are very open for discussion, a major culture change.

Here's an example of how the ABCs and our safety walkabouts created better supervisor-employee relationships, and improved safety as a result. We saw a guy exiting his vehicle improperly, so we gave him immediate feedback. He got very aggressive, yelling and waving his arms. The supervisor calmly listened. Then the guy cooled down and started giving us good suggestions on unsafe things we didn't even know about in his area.

The beauty of safety walkabouts is that we go, look, hear, listen, and take action.

SaFE℠ Observations

Safety for Everyone (SaFE℠) was a new way of tackling safety by working with front-line employees to give each other feedback, which they did not do under the old culture. With this new process, we were able to approach safety opportunities by asking, "How do we help each other be safe?" not "Why are they screwing up?" It was another application of Q4 Leadership℠. (See Figure 21.2.)

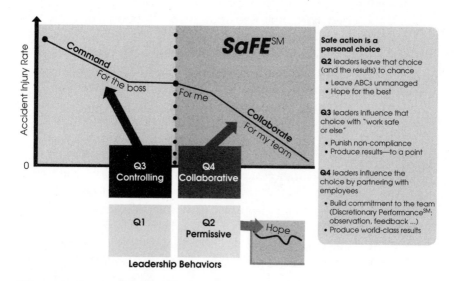

Figure 21.2   The SaFE℠ Curve
Source: The SaFE℠ Curve is a service mark of CLG.

Zero Tolerance and Why

Our focus on safety has been built on many personal stories from inside and outside the industry. We rely on leaders, as well as employees, to support one another in driving safe behavior.

Hunter knows firsthand the tragic end that failing to follow a safety regulation can have. Here he explains how he became passionate about safety, and why he demands 100 percent compliance every day:

> Everyone at CN knows I have zero tolerance for unsafe work practices. I insist that each and every one of us follow the rules with 100 percent compliance, 100 percent of the time.
>
> I know there are a lot of different opinions about this policy, but it's important that you understand where I'm coming from. There are simply too many accidents in this industry, too much pain and suffering that could be avoided if we just follow the rules. I know this firsthand, but I had to learn it the hard way.
>
> When I was a trainmaster on another railway, the shortest route from the yard office to the employee parking lot was a quick hop across a live track. There was a slightly longer path around the building, but a lot of people took the shortcut, even though the safer—and required—route was the longer one.
>
> I was in my office one Friday afternoon when a loud alarm and flashing blue light signaled that we'd just had a potentially fatal accident in the yard. I ran outside to find one of my co-workers lying on the tracks and covered in blood. He wasn't dead, but he was very seriously injured. His leg had been severed and was lying on the track beside him.
>
> How did this terrible accident happen?
>
> It happened because he'd ignored the rules and cut across the tracks on his way to the parking lot. Maybe his mind had been on the coming weekend, or maybe he'd just been tired. Whatever the reason, he hadn't noticed the group of cars rolling silently toward him—pushed from some distance away— that knocked him down, took his leg, and almost took his life.
>
> The saddest thing about this accident is that it could have been prevented. If he'd obeyed the rules and taken the longer route to the parking lot, he wouldn't have been in the wrong place at the wrong time.

I've seen too many people, at CN and elsewhere, make those little compromises that too often lead to such tragic results. That's why I'll never back down on this issue. We owe it to our employees, their families, and the company.

Zero tolerance may seem extreme, but bitter experience tells me that 100 percent compliance to safety 100 percent of the time is as critical to good railroading as any of the other Guiding Principles.

I've said many times that the rules are written in blood, the blood of those railroaders who let their guards down, didn't follow the rules, and paid a terrible price. But if I have anything to say in the matter, it won't happen on my watch.

(Adapted with permission from
How We Work and Why, **© 2005**
Canadian National Railway Company)

With safety tests, shift huddles, safety walkabouts, and SaFE^{SM} observations, we made progress in reducing personal safety incidents and injuries. More importantly, leaders and employees alike are involved in the process.

Still, some employees insisted on doing things unsafely. In a zero-tolerance culture, that leaves two choices: Do it safely, or do not work here. It is a continuous effort.

Success does not come from a single event. It comes from constant vigilance, and now we have everyone looking out for everyone else.

Sawing Our Way to Improvement

Today, we can build trains exceeding 200 railcars, powered by three locomotives. They stretch over 10,000 feet (around two miles). Such long trains are made possible by sophisticated technology and high-quality maintenance. How many railcars we actually include in a given train is controlled largely by economics and regulations.

In the days before we built such lengthy trains, two short trains could easily pass one another on a single track, using a siding, which is a short section of track built parallel to the main rail line as a place to park cars. Train A would drive onto the siding, train B would pass, and Train A would pull back out onto the main track to continue its journey.

But with some of today's trains nearly two miles long and many of our sidings less than half that length, we have a big problem when two trains meet on a single track and must get around each other.

One solution was to saw one of the trains in half. (See Figure 22.1.)

In the old days, we would have limited trains to 5,000 feet in length so they could easily pass each other. But running two 10,000-foot trains increases our cargo capacity by two-thirds, so we had to come up with a solution for when two trains must pass, which we did.

The moral: If you accept what you believe to be your limitations, you'll never become better. But if you tackle your limitations and devise workarounds, you'll improve.

That is how we improved our culture: thinking outside the box, sawing things in half, doing whatever worked.

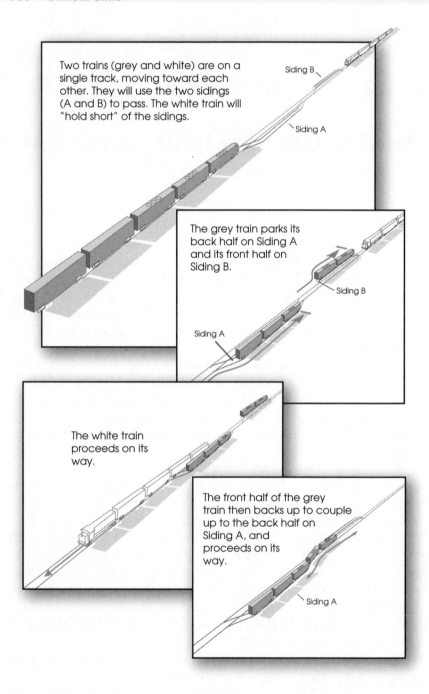

Two trains (grey and white) are on a single track, moving toward each other. They will use the two sidings (A and B) to pass. The white train will "hold short" of the sidings.

Siding B

Siding A

The grey train parks its back half on Siding A and its front half on Siding B.

Siding B

Siding A

The white train proceeds on its way.

The front half of the grey train then backs up to couple up to the back half on Siding A, and proceeds on its way.

Siding A

Figure 22.1   How to Saw a Train in Half
Source: CLG.

Tackling Old Problems in New Ways

In the new culture, we started tackling existing problems in new ways. People began asking, "Why are we doing it this way?" "If we can get that much change from focusing on behavior, what can we do if we improve the process first?"

This was process improvement in a new light: We could be creative because frontline leaders now had the power, skills, and decision authority to make their own process changes. Leaders no longer had to wait for their boss to mandate or approve something. They didn't have to wait for corporate to start new training or create a new initiative. Leaders could make the tough decisions because they had the best knowledge to make them.

This was part of our new culture. Each employee now had the authority and accountability to seek ways to improve his job, site, or business unit to better the business. Employees and leaders who were once afraid to make decisions were now expected to do whatever was needed to improve the business.

Reducing Overtime

"Overtime was one of our biggest problems," recalls Tom Evans, Assistant Superintendent of Transportation in Jackson, Mississippi. "Overtime cost a lot and we were using people inefficiently. Sometimes one crew would finish early while another was working overtime. It made no sense and strained the business and our employees' personal lives."

After our ABC training, we decided to tackle the overtime problem. "We used the 'Process Improvement Guide' from Hunter's book, *How We Work and Why,*" says Warren Porter, Baton Rouge Trainmaster. "CLG's consultant Jack Hinzman helped us use the ABC Toolkit to identify, pinpoint, analyze, measure, and coach." (See Figure 22.2.)

Dressed & Ready started about that time, and that helped reduce overtime just by getting everyone at work on time. Another key was telling everyone that we needed to reduce OT, because many had assumed it was okay.

Leaders often thought that employees wanted OT, but that wasn't the case. Our employees worked 10-hour days straight time before OT kicked in. Many of them told us they would rather

Process Improvement Guide

Some look at an operation and see opportunities and problems that others don't. How do they do it? They run through a checklist like this:

1. Look at each process in every area. Can you eliminate it?

2. Understand:
    a. What each step in a process does.
    b. How long it should take.
    C. What we're paying for each segment, part, and step.
    d. How many people are needed to accomplish the number of cycles, multiplied by the time per cycle = person-hours.

3. Ask people why we do it that way. If they say, "That's how we've always done it," you're on the right track. The process may not be understood and there may be room for improvement.

4. Now do two key things:
    a. Measure the process and its outcome: Be sure to use the right measures with data integrity (check where the numbers come from—wrong numbers will hurt you), and test the numbers—do they really measure what you want to measure?
    b. Give the process real attention. Measuring a process has no value if improvements suggested by the results don't receive attentive support.

5. Now look at each sub-component and say:
    a. We are going to do this cheaper, so let's figure out how.
    b. We are going to do this faster, with fewer resources and/or better service, so let's figure out how. (This is as much about attitude as intelligence, and where your measures really count. Does it take ten minutes to run that train down and switch it, or is it really seven minutes plus fluff or break time? Tap into your people's creativity—you may be surprised at what can be done.)

6. Set new expectations for each component you've looked at. Communicate them well and often, explain why they exist, and hold people accountable for achieving them. Use recognition and explain consequences to reinforce the changes.

7. Share what you learn with your colleagues at your location and others. It's not bragging—it's making sure we don't reinvent the wheel.

8. Most important: Do it now and move quickly—we can't afford to wait!

Figure 22.2   Process Improvement Guide

Source: Adapted with permission from *How We Work and Why,* © 2005 Canadian National Railway Company.

make a good daily rate and go home to their families. They even suggested ways to reduce OT.

Warren says, "Overtime was part of our ABC action plan, so we really focused on reducing it. We used the process to find changes that would reduce overtime. We lengthened our rail yard so we could have people working at both ends at the same time. We timed trains to arrive as others departed, so crews wouldn't wait for the next one to work on. And if crew A finished early while crew B would have to work over, we put crew A to work instead of having crew B stay over."

Warren reported a dramatic OT reduction. In the base year, weekly average OT was 45.5 hours. But the following year, OT during the corresponding period averaged only 18.0 hours, a 60 percent drop.

At our Jackson facilities, improvements went way beyond reducing overtime—there was a ripple effect giving us collateral benefits we had not foreseen. To reduce OT, we had to work more efficiently, and that made other things fall into place:

- Trains started running closer to on-time, improving our ability to deliver trains on schedule to 100 percent.
- By reducing overtime, we significantly reduced costs.
- Cars were running up to 24 hours earlier, allowing us to better manage and utilize our locomotives.

A fair question to ask is, "Were the ABCs entirely responsible for all of this improvement?" We believe that the ABCs were the primary influence, both directly (by promoting the right leadership and right behaviors) and indirectly (by creating an environment that encouraged everyone to improve how they worked).

Reducing overtime was a real team effort. Supervisors explained what they were doing and asked for support from the workforce. Everyone was included in the overtime assessment. Some of their ideas were used, and supervisors gave praise or coaching when needed.

Senior leadership helped by delivering consequences. Tom Evans says, "Our SVP, Gordon Trafton, calls us regularly, giving us feedback on our performance. Hunter saw the improvement in the terminals and took the time to call me, our Engineering Department, and our Mechanical Department. He told us that he saw what was going on, appreciated what we were doing, and asked us to share his thanks with the workforce. That made me feel really good."

"We share everything with our people now," Tom added. "The more they know about the job, the better they can do it. They see the bigger picture and there is less uncertainty. They don't just switch railcars around, but know where they are going."

Once we had a model that worked, we could share it across the company.

"Improve" Can Even Mean Tossing Old Paper Files

Daniel Gignac and Sherrie Summers of CN's People Department tell how thinking in a new way led to an opportunity to improve the way we manage employment files.

> Bureaucracy landed on our doorstep one day, with a huge thud.
>
> When our Disbursement Management Center was reorganized, its employees moved on. They had been responsible for employee files.
>
> But bureaucracy has incredible inertia, so the files continued to go to the Archive Centre. With no one to open, categorize, and file them, the envelopes overwhelmed the inbox. Someone piled them on the floor, but the pile toppled due to its height.
>
> One of our leaders asked us to solve the problem. We weren't in the same group, but he felt we had the talent to find a solution.
>
> We had not managed employee files for the past 20 years, but we had lots of support and a blank sheet to start with. So we changed entirely from paper files to electronic. This meant scanning the old files, which we had never done. There was no road map or budget, just employees who believed it was the right thing to do.
>
> We started with the critical asset utilization question: "What do we really need to keep?" Our HR colleagues and legal counsel gave us a list and we gathered files from every office.
>
> People we had never met called. "I have some boxes of employee files for you. Where should I send them?" The weirdest one was, "When do you want the ones in the mine shaft?"

Hunter was right about waste. A typical file contained 1 to 1.5 inches of paper, but only 10 pages were worth keeping.

In all, we scanned over 400,000 documents and got rid of 2,895 boxes or records. That's a stack over a half a mile high. The recycling alone must have saved a small forest!

In the end, it was just like having too many boxcars or locomotives. All the junk in our files was getting in the way of the information we really needed. Now getting an employee's file doesn't require several days' wait for it to arrive from a distant location. It takes 22 keystrokes and two seconds.

(Adapted with permission from *Change,*
***Leadership, Mud and Why,* © 2008**
Canadian National Railway Company)

Before we declared war on this problem, we had some 275,000 boxes of employee records companywide. Some thought this was a trivial problem, but they hadn't done the math: 275,000 boxes times $5 per box storage per year equals $1,375,000.

Unconvinced, someone noted, "You own some of the storage sites, so it's not a real cost." Oh? For one of the smaller sites that we recently cleaned out, we had signed a 20-year lease for $1.3 million a year plus utilities. The irony: The lease was to a records storage company.

Asset Utilization is as powerful for other companies as it is for CN. A major CN customer with a huge private fleet told us, "If you had offered in service and reliability 15 years ago what you offer today, we would have bought only half the 90,000 railcars we currently own. At $90,000 to $100,000 per railcar, that would be hundreds of millions in direct savings—even more if you consider reduced handling cost and repair."

Formalizing the Opportunity

What began as an opportunity for leaders to improve processes, creatively solve problems, and significantly change the business quickly grew into another opportunity for our team to help the organization take a significant step forward. It was another switchpoint in our journey.

PART VII

SPIKING THE SWITCHES

Through the process of changing the culture, we aligned several switchpoints, making decisions to move the company in a new direction, moving closer to our desired future state. For each of those decisions, we needed to spike the switch to ensure that the culture would continue forward and not fall back into old habits. To spike the switches, we put in place several changes in organizational systems and management processes to support the new direction.

23

Leadership Competencies to Support the Change

Our culture change was organic, developed primarily from the ground up. It was a corporate-inspired program, but we executed it through the field, customizing both content and deployment to the needs of each region.

So when we got ready to require leaders to demonstrate Q4 Leadership℠ behaviors, we had to ask, "Is everyone clear on those behaviors?"

Not surprisingly, the answer was no. In some areas, leaders had adopted new behaviors, but in others they continued to use leadership actions that had worked under the old culture.

Just before we started our partnership, CN had created a robust framework of leadership competencies for all levels of leadership, from executives through to first-line supervisors. This framework of role-based competencies was what we needed at the time it was developed.

However, as we changed the culture, leaders changed their behaviors. They started doing their own jobs instead of the jobs below them. They continued to move the bar so much that by 2006 the once-effective competency framework was out-of-date and needed to be replaced. As we progressed with the cultural change, the old competency framework grew farther away from the new role of the leader—the one that supported the new culture.

We now needed a structure with leadership skills, competencies, and behaviors to fulfill the new culture. The old behaviors (just five years old) were out-of-date because we had come so far.

Accountability and Importance

We clearly needed new competencies when we started holding people accountable for their behaviors. Until then, leaders didn't care what was in the leadership competency framework. They never used it because they were never told to, and their bonuses did not depend on it.

Now, not only were they being measured on their leadership behaviors for bonus evaluations, but they were also measured for promotions, accolades, and transfers. If you want to create focus on an issue, that's how to do it.

The New Competency Framework

We assembled a team of experts to review the competency framework (*experts* loosely meant a small group of HR and Operations folks, and a few external consultants). We had the common leadership competencies, which were still important for leaders:

- Commit to safety.
- Serve customers.
- Drive for results.
- Build relationships.
- Analyze problems, make sound decisions.
- Lead process improvement and change.

But these were not enough. We had to ensure leaders were promoted and recognized for competencies that truly added value at CN. So we added these new ones:

- *Influence and inspire.* Model a passion for the railroad and transportation business that motivates others to perform at high levels. Negotiate persuasively and build support for ideas by understanding and addressing others' priorities as well as your own.
- *Develop yourself and others.* Take ownership of your own development, seeking and acting on opportunities to improve

skills that deliver sustainable results. Give others feedback, coaching, and consequences to enhance their performance and contribute to CN's success.

- *Execute with excellence.* Set and provide direction based on comprehensive plans. Make sure people have the skills and resources to succeed. Create and reinforce clear measures of success and follow up to ensure they are met.

Next, for each level of development, we detailed two or three critical behaviors that a leader needed to perform under each category. (See Figure 23.1.)

Redefining the leadership behaviors brought clarity to all levels of leadership. Leaders now had clear alignment of expectations and

Competency	Executive behaviors	Senior manager behaviors	Manager behaviors	Supervisor behaviors	Individual contributor behavior
Commit to Safety	Models safe behaviors	Analyzes safety results	Offers safety improvement suggestions	Consistently monitors safety	Demonst sharp know safe
Serve Customers	Considers impact of customer solutions on entire system	Holds team accountable for follow-through	Maintains personal connections with key customer accounts	Consistently works to build and sustain relati	
Drive for Results	Establishes bold, aggressive goals	Conveys strong sense of urgency	Communicat urgency of initia		
Execute with Excellence	Identifies and prevents future problems	Tracks team progress against goals			
Analyze Problems, Make Sound Decisions	Makes sound, timely decisions	Cham unpop decisi			
Influence and Inspire	Shows others' input and feedba values				
Develop Yourself a Others	d				

Figure 23.1   Sample Leadership Competencies

Source: Adapted from Canadian National Railway Company materials.

consequences, and clear alignment between corporate programs and local expectations.

It was time to go the next step and align expectations and consequences for our unionized employees—through the performance review and bonus system.

Leadership Equals Bonus

In the fall of 2005, Gordon Trafton assembled the top 150 leaders of CN's Southern Region for a "Q4 Workshop." It was a retreat to think about how they were leading the company and to strategize ways to do it better. They solved operating issues, identified barriers to tear down, and planned for the next year. They talked about the critical need to lead by engaging employees in the business.

By meeting's end, Gordon announced that next year's manager bonus would be tied to results, as in the past—but 20 percent of it would now be tied to *how* leaders got results.

Southern Region leaders now had to deliver results by engaging employees for long-term success. At first, Gordon asked for each leader's candid example of how they achieved results. But eventually they would have leadership surveys and feedback processes that would let employees share how they thought their leaders were doing.

We had come full circle. We had leaders engaging in the right behaviors to drive employee engagement, which drove long-term, sustainable results. We had to deliver on short-term results, too, but our focus was on sustaining results once we got them. We challenged and rewarded our leaders to deliver and maintain results in their areas.

Just as Gordon laid the groundwork in CN's Southern Region, so did other regions and functions. The old bonus requirements were being shifted a little at a time, from purely results-dependent scores to bonuses that required demonstration of the right leadership behaviors. We put our money where our mouth was—linking to both results and behaviors.

With the shift in bonus requirements we saw another uptick in focus, effort, and determination by leaders. They knew what it would take to get their end-of-year bonuses, and they were determined to deliver.

The New Power of Performance Reviews

Like all companies, we use performance reviews for management staff. But the ABCs have converted this process from a pro forma duty to a robust lever for improving performance and rewarding good performers.

Clarke Trolley, an Intermodal Terminal Manager, and Tony Marquis, a General Manager, tell how performance reviews have changed:

> "Our old performance reviews were for the whole team," says Clarke. "They didn't tell individuals specifically what to do to succeed. That was before the ABCs. Today, the review process is dramatically different.
>
> "The ABCs taught us about pinpointing behaviors and giving positive and constructive feedback. We now build feedback on these skills right into our performance reviews. I'm seeing managers use them to drive business results, accountability, and personal development."
>
> Tony continues, "Before, we looked at these reviews for ten minutes, signed off, and got back to work—they were meaningless. Today, my first-line employees see real meaning in the process: What behaviors do I have to perform to meet my numbers? We are using the reviews to align everyone's behavior, top to bottom."
>
> "Our reviews reflect the Guiding Principles with objectives like 'No more than x incidents per year or per 100,000 miles of train travel,'" says Clarke, "and we list specific behaviors needed to meet that objective.
>
> "We've also added 'ABC competencies' or management behaviors that are essential for managers, like 'ability to deliver positive and constructive feedback to employees.' If a person performs these behaviors and meets the objectives, wonderful. If not, we write an action plan for the person to change their behavior.
>
> "Our performance reviews are about getting everyone to do their best. This affects all Five Guiding Principles.
>
> "Noncompliance with your review puts both your bonus and your supervisor at risk. Such consequences have driven significant change in individuals, the team, and bottom-line results."

Clarke says, Is it sustainable? Yes, and here's why:

1. We have very strong support from our senior VP and general managers, because they have seen the value of coaching and using ABC tools.
2. Instead of waiting for regular reviews, employees now get frequent feedback.
3. Today we are using the reviews as living documents, reflecting behaviors that people expect to see.

"Today, you cannot be a CN manager unless you use the ABC tools."

24

Performance Scorecards for Unionized Employees

Les Dakens had always been bothered by the lack of formal recognition for unionized employees at CN. The vast majority are great people who contribute a lot to our success. Yet we didn't take time with them individually to discuss what they achieved, nor did we take time to thank them for their efforts. In some cases, we knew that a number of employees had been given very little if any feedback for years.

The scope of this neglect was staggering. Of our 22,500 employees, 18,500 were unionized. This meant 80 percent were without any type of formal review! So the vast majority of our employees who were good contributors went without specific thanks. The 5 or 10 percent who needed to improve their performance went without coaching. Clearly, this was no way to move our culture.

It was time for action. We were going to make improvements and sweeping change. There would be no phase-in or multiyear rollout. It would happen this year.

For the first time in CN's 90-year history, every single employee was going to get a review. Thus was born the Employee Performance Scorecard (EPS).

Many found this revolutionary idea unthinkable as well as undoable. No one else in the rail industry—or most other industries—used scorecards for unionized employees. Reviews for unionized people were unthinkable because the employees were covered by a collective agreement. This tends to make leaders believe that straight talk about performance is risky.

Doing the Unthinkable

Yet it's funny how thinking the unthinkable can lead to change. As Les and Hunter flew to New York for an analysts' meeting in 2005 to celebrate the tenth anniversary of CN's IPO, they spoke again of Les's dream of Employee Performance Scorecards for unionized workers.

Even though it had not been done before, it was easy to see the value in EPS:

- Most unionized employees work hard and do a good job. It was right to recognize their contribution and thank them for it.
- The lifeblood of successful companies, and the fuel for future change, is inclusion and a shared understanding of goals, expectations, and priorities. Having another 18,500 people engaged in making us even more effective couldn't hurt!
- We have a big appetite for leaders, and the unionized ranks sported many bright, able employees. Performance reviews could be a vehicle for supervisors to further coach their people for their current jobs and toward future promotions.

So Hunter and Les decided that during the analysts' meeting, Les would announce that in 2006 every employee would receive a performance review, including unionized people. It was all part of helping employees do a good job, which would translate into improved company performance, which analysts always want to hear.

So Les addressed the analysts: "The new performance evaluations will be called EPS. To you in this room, that means *earnings per share.* But when you think about it, the individual performance of our employees is what adds up to make the company successful. So our new EPS stands for *Employee Performance Scorecards.* These scorecards will produce the other EPS, earnings per share. By growing one, we'll grow the other."

Executing EPS

Promising EPS was one thing; making it happen for 18,500 people within a year was quite another. It was not a scheduled Human Resources priority for the year. There was no staffing, funding, or detailed plan for design or delivery. HR bought the concept, but pulling it off would take a miracle.

When Les arrived back in Montreal, he went to Peter Edwards' office to break the news. Peter wasn't shocked by the concept. He had experience in the area, and he and Les had talked about it many times. But he certainly was startled by the timeline: It suddenly had been moved up two years earlier than planned! However, it had already been announced to the analysts, so we were off to the races.

Peter assembled the team and charted the course. Led by Christine Joanis and Susan Seebeck, they developed the scorecard and metrics, trained supervisors, and planned the rollout logistics. Although CLG had not been involved in developing EPS, their consultants assisted with implementation.

By the time EPS was finished, it would directly touch about 90 percent of CN's people. Of course, we anticipated that the unions would be concerned, so we needed a communication plan to give people a heads-up on EPS.

Communicating EPS

We wanted employees to have a good experience with EPS. Our goal was to start a meaningful conversation between the supervisor and employee on performance. Here are a few of the points we covered with each employee:

- We thanked them for their contribution to a successful organization (EPS is a vehicle that can help supervisors take time to say thank-you).
- We discussed their progress to date.
- We discussed the impact of their performance on the business.
- We discussed their opportunities to improve and advance.

So we needed to train the supervisors. They needed to be clear on EPS's purpose so they could explain it to employees. They would need some help with the feedback part, as not everyone had attended an ABC workshop. We put a training program together and piloted it in the field.

Then Came the Problems

Any change initiative will have problems, but this one was really asking for it.

- *Pushback from the unions.* As the buzz about EPS grew, the unions grew curious. Their chief concern was that EPS was going to be discipline in disguise, and they had strong and negative initial reactions.
- *A lack of common definition on measurements.* Senior operations leaders all identified their most important metrics. However, CN is actually an assembly of many different railways with multiple legacies of culture, union contracts, and leadership style. So while measurements might all have the same label (like *absenteeism*), they had different numerical values in each legacy railway.
- *Finding accurate performance data.* EPS required accurate data to track individual performance. But CN had multiple data sources, very few of which talked to each other. We had to find ways to get accurate data so the scorecard would prompt a discussion about individual performance instead of a debate on data accuracy.
- *Different versions for different needs.* Operations wanted to own the scorecard. There were many different jobs in the system, and opinions across the regions varied about what was needed. Demand mounted for multiple versions, so 48 unique styles of cards were developed for use across the organization, some in English, some in French.
- *Printing color scorecards.* The scorecard was to be given to employees as a tangible reminder of their EPS review. Supervisors would actually print the scorecards at their desks. But the scorecard needed the right look and feel, which led to doing it in color. With few color printers in the field, that meant planning ahead to print and ship from corporate.

The biggest surprise was the way so many supervisors viewed their jobs. To them, their job was getting the work done by assigning tasks—not supporting, developing, and coaching employees.

We planned to roll out EPS very soon and we fixed the problems fast. We revamped the training, with more emphasis on developing and motivating employees. We defined each measurement and added an explanation to each scorecard package. Where needed, we scrambled to identify each direct report for the supervisors.

Rollout for Success

The rollout happened on schedule. As is typical for CN, EPS was an idea developed centrally, then deployed regionally. Our small team, with other looming priorities at the start of the year, pulled off the massive undertaking in less than one year. We were done in December 2006. Our promise to the analysts was kept.

The employees' reactions opened many supervisors' eyes. The feedback held real meaning to employees. It was positive recognition that their contributions were important and appreciated. Some employees took their scorecards home and taped them onto the refrigerator!

For those supervisors who had the ABC training, EPS was the next logical step. Using the ABCs methodology, they were having discussions about performance and giving feedback to employees day-to-day. Now, with EPS, supervisors could pull together performance data and their observations from the year to have a meaningful conversation.

Supervisors learned that people needed to hear the details, and were actually hungry for them. The supervisors could also see the need to be clear in setting expectations, exact in defining measurements, and precise in choosing the right consequence for behavior.

After EPS was instituted at one rail yard, employees exceeded their goal of handling 340 railcars per shift by hitting the 360 mark. Intrigued by this productivity gain, Terry Corson, a Senior Mechanical Officer, asked yard supervisors what had changed. What new process had they instituted?

The answer: "The only thing changed at this location was the Employee Performance Scorecard."

Supervisors: I Didn't Know That!

EPS enabled supervisors to know their people in a different way, because it required conversation. Supervisors asked employees how it was going, discussed issues, and gave their perceptions about the employees' performance.

They got employees to talk about their experiences on the job, about the company, and what they thought about working there. And this enabled supervisors to learn some things:

- That some employees knew the customers and their needs better than they did.
- That employees had ideas about how to make the work more efficient, but often were afraid to share.
- That there were some practices that employees didn't understand well, or maybe just didn't like.

These conversations helped supervisors rethink how to do things. They were getting upward feedback for the first time.

Consultant Steve Quesnelle has a remarkable story about what one supervisor learned while conducting a one-on-one EPS session with a veteran employee in a mechanical shop in Winnipeg:

> When they came to the section on attendance, the supervisor congratulated the employee for having zero absences.
>
> The employee responded, "That's right. I've never had an absence."
>
> To which the supervisor replied, "Yes, that's great. You went the entire year without an absence."
>
> The employee smiled wistfully. "Actually, I haven't ever had an absence—not one day in 30 years."
>
> The supervisor nearly fell off his chair—partly from the enormity of this fact, and partly from embarrassment at not knowing this stunning fact and how dedicated this employee was.

EPS Was Another Switchpoint

EPS was coming on the heels of major cultural changes: the Five Guiding Principles, the ABC methodology, and the introduction of the Q4 Leadership℠ framework. EPS was a layer atop that existing foundation, and it was an informal test of how well CN had learned to put Q4 into action.

We saw a difference in how people responded to EPS. Of course, we got the usual comments from those who dislike change. But with EPS—a huge change that came from nowhere—we got some new reactions: "What do you need from me to make it work?" "Sounds like a plan, let's do it." It was obvious that our resiliency with change had grown.

We'll give the last word on EPS to our employees. Here's what they said:

> "For the first time I feel like I'm being heard."
>
> "This was a good discussion. Supervisors are changing. Previously, I always wanted to stay out of the superintendent's office. Now, supervisors have their door open."
>
> "I've been here 30 years and no one's ever thanked me before."
>
> "It's about time."

And although not a CN employee, French dramatist Victor Hugo perhaps said it best: "An invasion of armies can be resisted, but not an idea whose time has come."

CHAPTER 25

Learning through the Railroad MBA

Very few educational institutions teach anything about railways. Some teach logistics, international trade, and the like. But none of them teaches you how to unplug a jammed rail network, optimize a rail yard for efficiency, or put together a rail network strategy.

This created a continuing challenge for us. We'd bring in highly successful leaders from other industries, and they just weren't as effective here. They didn't understand the levers well enough to achieve what they wanted or we needed.

The Railroad MBA

So we created our own Railroad MBA (RR-MBA) program for selected senior executives. It is flexible, customized for each leader who takes the program. Participants learn how all the pieces intersect and get hands-on experience in operations. Or, if they already have operational experience, we expose them to sides they never see—sales, finance, and marketing. To date, we have had senior vice presidents of Operations and Marketing participate, as well as VPs of Labor Relations, IT, and Finance.

It's an intensive program that lasts up to a year. Every week, participants submit their observations and analyses to Hunter. Their senses sharpen. It is amazing what opportunities these new eyes find for us! The dollar value is in the millions.

And when they return, they approach their jobs differently. They see how their function contributes to the overall corporation, because they have a new awareness of the big picture, and the role of the Five Guiding Principles in everything we do.

The Railroad MBA is part of CN's competitive advantage. This led to an interesting call one day from a university: Who was handling the program for us? the caller asked. It seemed a competitor was interested and wanted to copy our program.

Our answer, that we're doing it ourselves, was a surprise to them. At one time we did hire traditional MBAs, but most of them didn't work out for us. They were interested in becoming CEO, but we were interested in them becoming railroaders first, maybe CEO later!

Railroader Undergraduate Programs

The success of the RR-MBA made us think about expanding it. Obviously it is too resource-intensive to have all 22,500 CN employees participate, but there had to be a way to help everyone understand the business of railroading.

The solution was our Railroader Trainee Program (RRTP) and the Railroader Certification. These expose people to new experiences that will help them understand today's complex railroads.

It is our sincere belief that all CN employees, regardless of function, must know the railroad and think of themselves as *railroaders*. The more accountants know about scheduling trains and repairing track, and the more mechanics know about the business side, the better everyone understands and communicates, letting us run a better railroad.

As retirements create more leadership openings, we need replacements. We're investing in programs to help us put railroaders in those leadership positions.

Any employee—sales account manager, marketing analyst, human resources manager, and so on—can become certified as a conductor (the on-train coordinator) and can then progress to be an engineer (train operator). What better way to understand the business than by driving the trains, meeting the customers, and seeing the problems and opportunities firsthand?

Our graduates go back to their jobs in IT, Finance, or Marketing, but they carry a new and better understanding of the railroad. That helps them see the bigger picture and make more informed

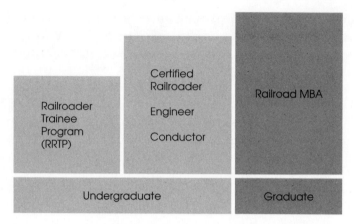

Figure 25.1   CN's Railroader Continuing Education Programs
Source: CLG.

decisions, as they realize that every decision in every part of the company touches some area of our system. (See Figure 25.1.)

CN Is a Destination, Not a Job

The train engineers and conductors have always thought of themselves as railroaders, but now so do our employees in IT, Accounting, HR, Marketing, Public Affairs, and all functions. All employees feel more connected to the enterprise. Their pride in being called *railroaders* is a signpost along our journey of culture change. It says our people are becoming deeply engaged in the business.

The basic requirements to work at CN are to be interested in your work, committed to the principle that we do what we say we will do, and be driven to make it happen. In shorthand, we call our employees *PHDs*: passionate, hungry, driven. They call themselves railroaders.

Not surprisingly, our largest source of new-hire referrals is our employees. They are shrewd judges of what it takes to be a railroader. They know it's not for everyone. Railroaders must consider the impact of everything they do on the whole rail network. As Hunter says, "Railroading is demanding on its good days."

Family referrals also help us recruit. It's not unusual for four or five generations of the same family to be employed with the company. Around the dinner table in many homes, you hear CN's stories told up close and personal.

Within our current workforce, as baby boomers begin to retire, we will lose much valuable experience. So we are encouraging people to pass on their knowledge and share the benefit of their experience. We want every employee to leave a legacy.

Today North America, Tomorrow the World

A measure of how far CN has come in only 15 years is that one investment analyst called us the Michael Jordan or Tiger Woods of railroading.

In Canada, you can tell how the overall economy is doing just by looking at our shipments. Our bills of lading are a bellwether for the Canadian economy.

Now we are building on what we have achieved—a railroad that interconnects an entire continent and two of the world's largest, most economically powerful countries. Our goal is not just to remain North America's best railroad, but to become the best *transportation* company in the world. Today it may be a dream, but with our culture and programs shaping strong leaders, we will have the railroaders—really, the transportation experts—to bring the dream to life.

With continually evolving programs and aggressive recruitment, we are confident we will be able to continually develop to meet future needs.

Hunter Camps Develop Leaders

About 18 times a year, Hunter meets with a group of 20 to 24 management people for three days. They go off-site, turn off their cell phones and pagers, and just focus on a few topics. These retreats, called *Hunter Camps*, are another example of Hunter's visible support and sponsorship for the new culture.

He began the camps in 2003 to communicate his Precision Railroading model to leaders in CN's Transportation Department. He soon added the Five Guiding Principles and how to use them in running our business, and his audience began to broaden to other CN departments.

Then he turned to leadership, especially of the culture change we were preparing, and that has become the camp's focus today. His message is straightforward, timeless, and simple: *It is impossible to change and improve business without people who lead well.*

Hunter repeats and underscores this over and over, using many stories from his years on the railroad. By the end of camp, people get it: CN is changing, and they are expected to help lead that change.

Hunter Camps are unique to CN. What other organization has its CEO spend 54 days a year with groups of managers who come from all functions and levels in the company? This was, and still is, a critical aspect of how we are revolutionizing our culture at CN.

Expanding the Impact

When Hunter Camps began, the audience consisted of up-and-coming young managers in transportation, nominated by senior leaders and designated as high-potentials. These people were CN's future, growing to become the organization's leaders for many years to come.

As we developed the camps, we broadened the participant list. Every employee across CN impacts our business, so Hunter's thinking about leadership and how to run a railroad is relevant to everyone. We added people from every function companywide—Operations, Finance, Information Technology, Human Resources, Sales, and so on.

The scope of the camps shifted as we learned more about what participants wanted and needed. Early camps lasted a day and a half. Then we added other topics and deepened the emphasis on leadership. Now they run three days.

Over time, four camps a year blossomed to 18, with a plan to reach 1,800 leaders within CN. This is a very serious investment in everyone's future.

Although connecting with only 24 campers in each session (which makes 432 leaders a year that Hunter works with personally), Hunter reaches many more people indirectly. All of these leaders take home new thinking and spread it to their teams.

And there is another benefit to all: Hunter insisted that Les Dakens or Peter Edwards attend each camp, not only to help facilitate, but to help identify up-and-coming talent for the organization.

Learning from the Master

A Memphis native, Hunter is a master of the Southern tradition of storytelling. As he tells his tales—all true—campers listen intently. The issues are serious, Hunter's passion is contagious, and it's entertaining as well.

Campers learn firsthand about railroading and leadership from the man named "Railroader of the Year" by *Railway Age* in 2002 and "CEO of the Year" by Toronto's *Globe and Mail* in 2007. They learn what is expected of them and what behaviors they need to demonstrate. But at a deeper level, Hunter is *teaching participants how to think* about the business. Information is useless if you don't use it.

Through his stories, he presents many ways to apply the Five Guiding Principles.

The camps are very much a two-way street. Every camp devotes time to exploring real-life challenges that campers face on the job. Hunter listens to issues and problems and offers ideas and suggestions, explaining his thinking.

It's not theory, it's real life—and the campers enjoy a privileged view of Hunter's way of approaching, analyzing, and solving dozens and dozens of problems that get posed during their three days together.

Hunter makes clear that not everything will be easy: "There is no magic bullet or secret formula for leadership. It's all about hard work. Few want to hear that."

Twelve Characteristics of Leadership

One of the biggest challenges for the camps is addressing the range of generations that each leader manages. Hunter relies on teaching from consultant Morris Massey[1] to help campers understand the differences across the generations. Then he goes further by discussing how best to lead them.

By each camp's end, participants have learned pragmatic leadership lessons that aren't in management books:

- Leadership is about disciplined thinking that rests on courage, passion, and integrity.
- Leadership is making tough calls when you know you're doing the right thing.
- Leadership is knowing when to lead, when to follow, and how to be part of the team.
- Leadership is knowing how to be a champion for a cause, person, or principle you believe in.

Campers learn these lessons by discussing Hunter's Twelve Characteristics of Leadership:

1. Think deeply about your plan and communicate it effectively.
2. Lead from the front of the train (set the example).
3. Know how to follow.
4. Make the tough calls.

5. Deal with conflict and performance issues immediately, straightforwardly, and toe-to-toe.
6. Develop people.
7. Have high personal integrity and insist on it with others.
8. Know your people.
9. Have passion and inspire it in others.
10. Champion your people.
11. Listen to your people—and hear them.
12. Get results!

For many campers, outlining these 12 characteristics is handing them keys to problems they've wanted to solve for years. Campers hear these messages:

- It matters that you care about what you do.
- Whether your style is quiet or center stage, the real key is wanting the company to succeed, then figuring out what success looks like and how to get there.
- CN has room for different styles and a need for different viewpoints, as long as everyone agrees on the goal of improving the business.

Leadership Is about People

Hunter's leadership message is simple: "Leadership is about people. People are assets, not liabilities. If you unleash the power of people, it's amazing what can be done."

It's an excellent example of our Continuum of Engagement in operation. Hunter advocates getting as many people to the "engaged" end of the continuum as is possible—he wants their Discretionary Performance^{SM} to help CN be great.

Though widespread, his message of engagement and sound leadership is not yet common culture throughout our railroad. It's admittedly not what some people experience in their workplace. It's not always what they hear from their bosses, and they may not yet be rewarded consistently for engaging people. But with each Hunter Camp, the old culture breaks open a bit more. Each camp shifts the culture a little further.

With the success of the camps, we expanded them to include a surprisingly broad cast of characters, including CN's customers, union leaders, and recently even leaders from competing rail lines. What we talk about is no secret, and we freely hand out our book, *How We Work and Why*, to anyone interested in running their organization better.

Is this giving away the store? Not at all. What makes CN so successful is not the content of the book and the camps—it is CN's ability to *create exceptional leaders who know how to execute.*

Some Campers' Views

When people finish camp, many write unsolicited comments to Hunter about their experience. Their notes contain reflections on the key messages they have taken away from camp, and stories about what they have done to apply their learnings in their jobs.

The stories vary from encouraging to some that bring tears. Every camper has a tale to tell, and many have quantifiable results to share:

- "Watching the camp format allowed me to improve my own leadership style by asking more questions, listening, asking what the person recommends, and explaining my own decisions if we differ. All in all, it makes for a better approach."
  —*Keith Bonnyman, Assistant Comptroller, Non-Freight Management*
- "I'm back from Hunter Camp, all boosted and motivated. Hunter is an eloquent speaker and a real businessman. His stories and knowledge are remarkable. My takeaways: Passion is contagious; leaders have great influence over their peers and staff; go back to basics and use your business sense."
  —*Jean-Francois Boudreau, CPA*
- "My learnings: Do it now and fix the process; if you engage others you have an even greater impact; be safe. I can see Hunter with his red marker, stabbing at the flipchart, pointing at me, circling, displaying his unwavering beliefs in these themes." —*Jennifer Marvin, Senior Manager, Customer Interactions, Business Integration*
- "Hunter Camp made me realize that change management is of utmost importance and is fully supported at the highest executive level, our CEO. Hunter is ready to take us 'out of the mud' if we need his help solving our challenges. We're

very successful, but we need to regularly reconsider how we do things." —*Benoît Marcil, Taxation*

- "I took away a real sense of momentum in transforming our culture. I understand better where CN is going and what it needs from me. I always tell my team, 'We're not accounting people who work for a railroad, we are railroaders who work in Accounting.' Hunter Camp made me feel like a true railroader." —*James Harrington, Senior Manager of Automated Invoicing*

- "I didn't expect Hunter to dedicate so much time to us. Such action shapes CN's culture. It inspires us as leaders that going beyond expectations motivates others to do the same. My key takeaway is that as a leader I have the opportunity to influence and motivate others and help shape the culture at CN." —*Robert Staric, SOX Project Leader*

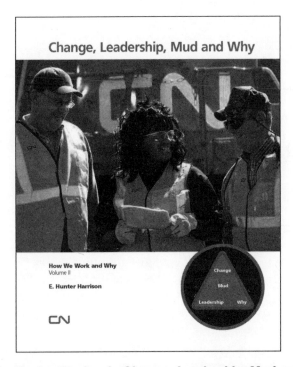

Figure 26.1   Hunter Harrison's *Change, Leadership, Mud and Why*

Source: E. Hunter Harrison, *Change, Leadership, Mud and Why,* © 2008 Canadian National Railway Company.

The camps have grown along with our culture change—but have they helped change our culture? We think so. Hunter is doing it by influencing leaders at all levels in the best way possible: face-to-face. He is giving permission and encouragement to engage with the change, direct from the top.

And there is responsibility on the part of campers as well. Six months after attending, they are required to submit a page on how they have used what they learned and the results they have achieved.

Hunter's 2008 book, *Change, Leadership, Mud and Why*, shares his key concepts and many stories from the Hunter Camps. (See Figure 26.1.)

Hunter Camps are part of the visible sponsorship of change from our CEO—sponsorship experienced personally or heard from someone who attended camp.

The Power of Consistency
(17 out of 17)

Armed with the ABC Toolkit and a deeper knowledge of the Five
Guiding Principles, our leaders were ready to change the culture—
except for one thing. To truly drive culture change, *we needed to provide
consistent consequences from consistent leaders.* This realization became a
switchpoint in our cultural change.

In a relay race, it doesn't matter how well three runners do,
even if they are the fastest on the track. If the fourth runner drops
the baton, the race is over for the whole team. For the same reason,
consistency in culture change is essential to winning.

While consistency seems like an obvious requirement, it took a
small group of managers 12 hours of discussion to really grasp its
impact, as revealed in this story from our recent history:

> We slumped in a meeting room late one night amid empty
> pizza boxes and soda cans, tired to the bone. We had been at
> this since 7:30 that morning, and had been on this grueling
> schedule for weeks. We were desperately trying to change the
> out-of-control elements of our railroad—early quits, theft, low
> productivity.
>
> That night it finally dawned on us: *We, the leaders, were the
> problem.*
>
> Too many of us were inconsistent in our expectations of
> employees. Some of us let people leave early, overlooked theft,

or didn't ask people to do their best. We thought we were being good guys.

If we didn't stop overlooking these actions, then and there, CN was headed for a dead end. There would be no need to continue, as there would be no way we could change the culture.

So we took a simple oath: *No one dodges responsibility. We accept our role as leaders, and this is what we signed on for. And we will hold each other accountable for doing the right thing.*

There were 17 of us at that table. Someone said, "We all must agree—all 17 of 17 must align." That phrase stuck. From that point on, whenever the going got tough, we'd look at one another and say, "17 out of 17."

The mantra *17 out of 17* was catchy—an icon for consistency, performance, accountability. It spread like wildfire through the organization.

Every leader had been in a situation that created inconsistency and knew the pain it caused. The leader might have been the bad guy, the good guy, or even stuck in the middle. It didn't matter—they all recognized the issue. Through the ABC workshops, they saw the confusion that inconsistency brings to employees.

We identified two kinds of inconsistency: inconsistency in the rules, and inconsistency in applying them.

Inconsistency in the Rules

We know from the ABC methodology that antecedents (rules, expectations, policies) must be clearly aligned with the right consequences if they are to work. Employees are smart—they can see when the consequences they receive don't align with managers' expectations.

When employees see this inconsistency, they decide it's all right to ignore the rules. We found this to be true on several occasions, including the following:

Antecedent: Our rule says "Arrive at meetings on time."

Behavior: People drifted in later each week—first two minutes late, then five, then ten.

Consequences: Nothing was said about it. In fact, sometimes we waited for latecomers before we started meetings.

Result: The consequences didn't align with the antecedent, so employees made their own rule: "Show up when you feel like it."

Antecedent: "No entry" signs were posted in hazardous areas.

Behavior: People ignored the signs and took shortcuts through the areas.

Consequences: Nothing was said about it. And those who took the shortcut usually got where they were going faster than if they had obeyed the signs.

Result: "No entry" signs were ignored so often that it became common practice to walk right past them. Employees made their own rule: "Those signs must not apply anymore—no one bothered to take them down."

To make things worse, when we hire new employees, we pair them with experienced old hands to give them on-the-job training. The old hands tell them, "Forget the handbook, that's not how we do it—let me show you the real way."

Once a culture creates this second tier of real expectations and rules, you have lost the battle. You have widespread inconsistency between antecedents and consequences, meaning that you have lost control of behavior—people will do things their own way. At CN, this inconsistency was another switch we needed to spike.

Inconsistency in Applying Rules

Sometimes the consequences are clear, but they aren't applied in the same way every time by every leader. This is where *17 out of 17* comes in. If even one leader bends the rules for someone, he is creating inconsistency that can multiply and bring progress to a halt.

Employees see these inconsistencies (you do, too) and try to figure out when the consequences will be in their favor (you do, too). Do you have to do something only when Joe is on duty? Or only in the north side of the rail yard? Or only during day shift? Many companies have tales of how lax night shift is, compared to day shift, or how lax one supervisor is compared to others. All these observations get tucked away in employees' heads as they try to make sense of their unclear work environment.

These inconsistencies are bad enough, but there's more. Employee time spent in figuring out the system is lost time. Often, inconsistency drives so much grumbling and discussion among co-workers that employees lose many hours of productivity. These employees are not bad—they are normal people trying to make sense of their inconsistent work environment.

Inconsistency Breeds Opportunity

When things are inconsistent, the negative leaders step up—they smell an opportunity to make their own decisions about expectations and rules. This is where *17 out of 17* comes in again: If even one manager is lax, people who work for the other 16 begin to resent the special treatment they see some employees receiving. The negative leaders pounce on the opportunity to spread dissent.

The neutral majority who struggle to follow the rules but don't see their value will see this as an opportunity to take advantage of the system. They will take the opportunity to get away with what they know is the wrong thing to do.

If you have just one manager who allows just one employee to break the rules, the floodgates open. "Hey, if Sally can do it, then so can I!" "And me, too!" "And me!" The flood races forward and the management team is left to deal with managing rules instead of managing performance.

Leaders who fail to consistently enforce the rules create lifelines for bad actors, enabling them to get away with breaking the rules. Here is an example, told by one leader:

> Inconsistency provides shelter and encouragement to negative leaders. For example, negative leaders often find one manager they can get along with. Such a manager then becomes a lifeline to that negative leader, one who listens and even helps them when they need a favor.
>
> Here is a simple test I use to discover who is serving as the lifeline for a negative leader. When we have a culture problem, I gather the managers and ask, "Okay, who's the negative leader among our employees?" Pretty quickly, everyone agrees that it's Sue—everyone except Pat. He says, "I don't know why the rest of you are having problems with her. Sue's okay with me."
>
> A-ha! Pat is likely the lifeline for Sue.

So if you are the only person in the room that Joe seems to be okay with, you might be Joe's lifeline. You're the person Joe keeps for when he needs things. Joe probably doesn't work directly for you, but he's figured out that he can have everyone else angry with him, be a terrible employee and co-worker, and it doesn't really matter—he has you.

The real ability to get a negative leader to do the right thing comes when the lifeline manager truly embraces the concept of *17 out of 17* and tells the negative leader, "We have a good relationship, but I'm no longer going to be your source of help and favors in the future. You treat me well but you don't treat the other managers well. You sneak out early on them, and you don't treat your job with respect. When you don't do right for them, you don't do right for me either."

Now the negative leader has no lifeline, no shelter—and just as important, the recognition and positives are reserved for employees who do the right thing, not those who abuse.

The negative leader no longer gets undeserved rewards. He now must make a conscious choice: Am I willing to change, or live without someone to help me? Good employees see that we are serious about what we say. Over time, we create a consistency of consequences that people can count on.

So consistency on rules, policies, and procedures is the basic foundation for a strong management team. Once you have consistency, you can focus on *performance*—and helping employees maximize their abilities. Without consistency, leaders are wasting time dealing with basics that never give them time to deal with greater things.

Does size matter? Regardless of how big our management team became, or how spread out we were, we drove *17 out of 17* in every dialogue with them. It was just as critical for two people sitting in an office as it was for the team of 12 managing rail lines between Chicago and Memphis.

Be Consistently Flexible

One caveat: Consistency doesn't mean being inflexible. Being inflexible means that thinking has stopped and that policy is being used as if it were set in stone, or is being used as an excuse. If someone suggests a change, you can discuss it with others and approach the person: "I've heard your request and I talked about it with the others, and we collectively agree that it's okay."

That's part of the commonsense approach we are building across CN. Our good people should be able to expect recognition and that we will deal with those who choose not to help.

This is why we ask each manager to behave in a *17 out of 17* manner. As Hunter noted, some have said they can't. These people can still work for us—they just can't lead.

CHAPTER 28

Developing Internal Consultants

To truly live the culture change, we knew that CLG's coaching could not last forever. We needed to develop the capability to coach and support our leaders in-house. We set out to develop a cadre of internal consultants. Formal use of internal consultants did not begin until two years into our culture change.

Why Internal Consultants?

We started with a team of 45 committed—although lonely—owners: the executives, the HR group, and CLG. We worked hard to determine the need, create the process to execute change, and start rolling it out. Our band of executives and coaches owned the culture change.

But we were not the ones who made it come to life day-to-day. For this, we enlisted our superintendents, trainmasters, yardmasters, and everyone who worked daily to get the trains out on time. Only then would the culture change be *sustainable*.

We knew what we needed to do—but we needed the time to do it right. We were asking for major change from our leaders and employees, and we had to overcome a long history of negative consequences. We had to ensure that:

- People who spoke up were listened to.
- Our leaders followed through on what they said with rewards or discipline.

- Employees who worked hard were recognized.
- Employees who bent the rules no longer got away with it.

Culture change is about changing everyday behaviors across the organization. Basically, it is changing habits, and we all know how tough that is. It takes time and a lot of effort. Culture change is a multiyear process.

Transitioning from CLG to Internal CN Consultants

Our focus was always on developing strong leaders who were trained in the ABC methodology—the skills needed to make the culture change. But we also knew our busy leaders needed support to keep refreshed, to take on more complex projects, and to help develop their teams. To support our leaders long term, we had to build our own competency in-house: internal consultants who were skilled in the ABCs and culture change.

It's very tricky to transition work from the expert team that has lived and breathed the change, to a broader team that has to take ownership of it. If done too fast, we would put leaders in a position to fail, not succeed. (See Figure 28.1.)

Typically, project teams have a short window of time to transition to the line organization. Understanding the science of behavior, we knew we needed more time to ensure that the internal consultants

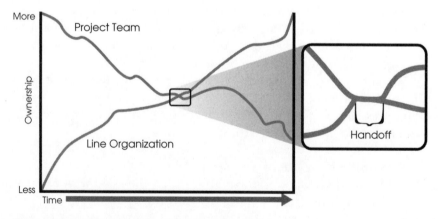

Figure 28.1   Transitioning Ownership
Source: CLG.

were ready to take the lead. We needed to create a handoff time of 6 to 12 months.

Selecting the Right People

We developed a curriculum to train internal consultants across the organization. We selected people from Operations, Human Resources, and Labor Relations.

We sought those who were knowledgeable about CN, and who had the passion and credibility to ensure leaders were supported in creating the new culture. Candidates had to be credible and respected among CN's business leaders, know enough about the organization to be helpful, have interest in and capacity to learn the ABCs, be good communicators, and have the strength to build relationships and coach leaders at any level. Sounds like we were seeking Superman and Superwoman!

Indeed, finding these individuals was a challenge, and then pulling them away from their regular jobs was all but impossible. But we did it. We made the commitment to develop the skills internally and we delivered on that commitment.

We started with a group of 13, all from the HR Department. They came from across the organization and each had strong relationships with operations leaders.

These coaches weren't picked because of their zip codes or because their plates were half full. They were chosen because they had demonstrated their worthiness to become coaches and confidants to the operations leadership team. In fact, when we asked the leadership team who would be good coaches, these were the people they selected.

Developing Internal Consultants

CLG and CN developed a customized "Internal Consultant Development Process." This process delivers:

1. Individual skill assessment and development planning to ensure steady progress.
2. Training to provide the necessary level of skill development and application.
3. Development events in which ABC coaches use their new skills to coach leaders for desired changes in behaviors

and results. Development events apply the learning and are key to success.

Internal consultants were certified at multiple levels of consulting skills and competencies. We needed most internal consultants skilled to coach and train managers.

After initial training, this group began an apprenticeship, coaching leaders alongside their CLG counterparts. Not only did they learn more about how to apply the tools, they also made gains in leader development and business results.

Reality Hits

The initial class of internal consultants was a big hit. Executives were so convinced of the need to develop internal coaches—and the ability of this particular group of people—that they asked for more to be trained. There was only one problem: We did not have the funding to train more consultants.

We went back to the executives to explain our situation. They were so confident in the process they were willing to pick up the tab for the training program. That speaks volumes for the value and trust that they placed in these internal coaches.

If cost was our first problem, time was our second. Operations leaders wanted us to train another 75 internal consultants, but they could not guarantee that these additional consultants would be available to coach and support leaders beyond their own work groups. They wanted local coaches—experts for their area who could take on a consultant role without leaving their normal day jobs.

When the request came through, Judy and Peter put their heads together to determine how they could create the role the Operations leaders requested. Out of this unique need was born the practitioner role.

Practitioners were trained in skills similar to the internal consultants, but maintained their current role and responsibilities. They received six days of additional leadership training and were charged as the "ABC champion" for their area. This meant they could use their newfound skills to help their teams develop projects and solve everyday problems. Practitioners were looked to as experts, people who prompted the team to use the tools and support the leaders through the process.

During the following two years, we trained, coached, and certified more than 80 internal coaches and practitioners. Creating a workforce of internal coaches is serious business, requiring time and restructuring to make it successful. Practitioners, coaches, and CLG consultants worked closely with one another and with operations leaders to change the culture, one behavior at a time.

These internal coaches and practitioners were sprinkled throughout the organization, continent-wide. (See Figure 28.2.) We

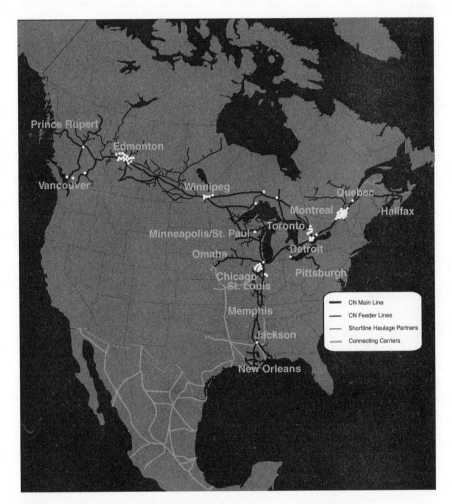

Figure 28.2 White Dots Show Deployment of Coaches and Practitioners throughout CN

Source: Canadian National Railway Company and CLG.

relied on them to function as spark plugs to ignite change from the bottom up. At the same time, we continued to support top-down leadership alignment to push the culture change.

As we progressed, we successfully transitioned leadership support in many areas. CLG stepped back from a direct role with supervisors to supporting internal consultants who now worked with the supervisors.

Unfortunately, this was not an exact science. There was no pre-planned timeline, no magic point to commence or complete the transition. We relied on the progress each leader was making and their comfort/ability to move forward without support from CLG's consultants.

Tony Marquis, General Manager of the Champlain Division, shares his thoughts:

> At first I thought, "This internal consultant business is such a waste." But then I realized that this is the most important thing that we are doing in this company.
>
> New supervisors take the basic ABCs course and work with an internal consultant. But learning to walk the talk was done with the practitioners, because they were on the front line and working side-by-side with the new leader.
>
> As we model and mold more people into the ABCs and become much more proficient, the structure is going to guarantee progress. It is going to stay—because CN has said this is the way we are going.

The Value of Internal Consultants

Internal consultants accelerated our culture change. They helped us go faster, broader, deeper, more cost-effectively, and with greater long-term sustainability. Many of the results in this book were accomplished by leaders working with internal consultants.

They have a unique role in changing an organization's culture. They are there when business leaders make decisions, push projects, and manage performance. Internal consultants work with the CLG consultants, continuing to learn and adapting those learnings for CN.

Internal consultants and practitioners are part of CN's future. They will help bring new leaders up to speed on the tools and leadership behaviors most critical to our high-performance culture.

They will help existing managers and leaders become more fluent in the tools and facilitate teams through tough situations. They have a responsibility and the tools to help every employee accomplish the company's goals and get results.

Some CN leaders still request external coaching help with major changes or on issues that need an outside perspective. That need may never go away. Like the culture, the CLG/CN partnership is evolving, with each company playing its part to make change happen—and make it stick.

29

Sustaining Culture Change

If changing a culture is hard work, sustaining it is even harder (just like most people who lose weight gain it back). Culture change is no different from exercising or breaking a bad habit: The first hump is a dramatic push in which you attain your goal, but the second hump is *keeping your success.*

Preventing Backsliding

Steve Serio, a CN Terminal Manager, tells a story about risk management in Chicago. It's about how we fixed a problem—we thought—then backslid, and then came back and really fixed it. It's about a leader's ability not just to make a change, but to monitor progress and work with his team to make adjustments in order to continuously improve. He said:

> Intermodal shipping containers like the one shown are everywhere—on tractor-trailers, in terminals, and on hundreds of CN's trains. (See Figure 29.1.) These containers lead a rough life. And when one is damaged, the responsible party pays for repairs.
>
> CN's inspectors reduce this liability by spotting existing damage on containers as they arrive by truck at our terminal. If we don't catch it, and accept a damaged container as okay, we become liable for repairs, increasing our costs.
>
> Any unwarranted cost, such as unnecessary repairs, is an offense to CN's Five Guiding Principles. Anytime we can reduce

Figure 29.1 Intermodal Containers in a CN Rail Yard
Source: Canadian National Railway Company.

unnecessary costs safely, that savings drops straight to the bottom line.

As incoming containers pass by video cameras, our inspectors sit in a booth, checking the containers on monitors. Yet in the first half of 2004, CN had the highest container liability of any rail line in Chicago. We identified very little damage and were losing $4,000 to $5,000 a month.

Then a CN team used the ABC tools. They guided inspectors to do a better job observing, identifying, and recording damage, and provided training to improve their video observations. Inspectors began capturing about six times more damage. CN quickly went from worst to best in Chicago.

We continued these great results for 12 months. But in May 2005, things began to backslide. We were not sustaining the change. We knew there had to be a better way. We applied the ABCs again—this time with one very important change: a change in behavior. In addition to using cameras, inspectors were now walking around trucks as they arrived in order to make a physical inspection, helping them identify damage that was not always visible on their monitors.

This change generated major bottom-line results: We went from the original six-fold improvement to a fifty-fold improvement, exceeding $250,000 in savings monthly. (See Figure 29.2.)

Employees now decide whether to physically inspect trucks in addition to using cameras. Supervisors give the inspectors encouraging feedback, and employees have taken the lead in maintaining this important savings trend.

The ABCs helped change the Chicago Yard's team to be better performers and leaders—and improved damage liability by an astonishing quarter-million dollars a month—in just one location.

This story is also an example of how powerful the behavior of *listening* can be. Middle management was frustrated with the performance plateau they hit. Then they heard an operator comment, "If we really want to catch all the defects, we need to get out and walk around the trucks ourselves."

How simple! No rule prevented operators from leaving the booth—just years of an ingrained practice, where they sat and used cameras to catch what they could. Leaving the booth did mean

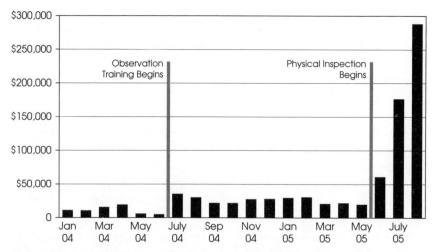

Figure 29.2 Average Monthly Damage Savings in Chicago Intermodal Rail Yard

Source: Adapted with permission from Braksick, *Unlock Behavior, Unleash Profits,* second edition (McGraw-Hill, 2007).

slowing down the inspections, but it also meant doing a better job, and saving more per year.

It simply took a few words from an employee, and a manager who listened. *That's how you create change, and sustain it.*

Techniques for Sustaining Change

What techniques sustain change? In our experience, here are the big four:

1. *Communication.* Communication is crucial for leaders whose employees are not as vigilant as they could be. These leaders must keep expectations clear and feedback channels open to ensure the organization catches and acts on setbacks.

2. *Alignment and accountability.* Maintaining alignment top-to-bottom helps leaders ensure that all employees are pulling in the same direction, working toward the same goal. Leaders also must hold people accountable for their part in delivering the results—both when they succeed and when they fail. It takes both alignment and accountability to sustain any culture change. With only one, you cannot drive continuous improvement.

3. *Manage with metrics.* We use metrics to track progress—progress against business results, and progress of the behaviors most critical to get those results. This way, if we see changes in the behaviors, we have an early warning sign that the results will turn as well.

4. *Arrange consequence systems.* Leaders must set up processes and systems to support the right behaviors. They must encourage getting results through actions that are aligned to the culture, and discourage actions that are not aligned. These are part of the fabric of the organization that delivers consequences to employees. If the systems do not support the change, it will slowly die. For example, supervisors can give positive feedback or use CNAP Cards (the CN Appreciation Program) to reward people for exceptional effort.

To be blunt, we've found that sustainability is and always will be hard work. It is all about holding the course, being observant for deviations from the plan, correcting when needed, and celebrating when successful.

Examples of Sustainability

Throughout this book we have shared real examples of what CN people did to sustain the culture change, including:

- Revising hiring practices.
- Succession planning.
- Leadership competencies.
- Employee Performance Scorecard (EPS) process.
- Process improvement.
- Hunter Camps.
- Railroader Certification.

In addition, we instituted annual awards for employees who demonstrate the behaviors we are seeking in the new culture.

- *President's awards.* These are very special awards for special people who have developed and implemented ideas that make a difference for the business. Recipients can be unionized employees, corporate staff, managers, teams, or individuals. Awards are given for such categories as Best Five Guiding Principles Initiative, Best Rail Yard, and so on.
- *Service awards.* Many companies have discontinued these, but CN is a destination employer. Some of our employees have stayed for 40 years, and we encourage long tenure. For every five years of service, we show appreciation with a gift. Our unionized employees are the best-paid railroaders in the industry. In most of our union agreements, we have guaranteed job security for existing employees. In return, we have flexibility to make changes needed to improve our business.

As we said, keeping a change going is even tougher than making it in the first place. We changed our culture dramatically over the past decade so that we could survive as a public company.

And now it will change even more, because CN can't become the best *transportation* company (not just the best railroad) in the world by remaining where we are today. To survive and prosper, we must become a company that unanimously believes in constant and unrelenting pursuit of improvement. CN is damn good, but we aren't there yet.

CHAPTER 30

Sharing Our Story

In all industries, changes in one company affect another. That is especially true of railroads because they are interconnected. We rely on other railroads to work with us to move our customers' freight— so they are both competitors and partners.

For example, CN cooperates with its main competitor, Canadian Pacific, to gain efficiency. There are places where the two railroads run parallel to one another, each operating on its own single track, side-by-side. Traditionally, each railway would invest capital to build sidings so one of its trains could park while another of its trains, coming from the opposite direction, could pass through, avoiding the two trains meeting on the single track. This created a potential safety hazard, increased costs, and increased transit time. The two companies agreed to share their tracks. For example, they cooperatively scheduled trains so that both companies' eastbound trains would share one set of tracks and both companies' westbound trains would share the other set.

At CN, we initiated many of the changes in the railroad industry. But some of it happened *to* us, because of changes happening elsewhere. It feels better when we lead the change, but when it comes at us, we must deal with it.

As we improved our culture, some of the changes involved our customers, suppliers, and competitors. We gladly share what we've learned the hard way with all of our partners, because it helps them and ultimately helps us too. And we're very open to learning from others and adopting their best practices.

Sharing with Our Customers

Most of the change that our customers have experienced has been positive. Through becoming a Precision Railroad, we moved their shipments on their schedule, not ours. More reliable service and shorter transit times have been winners both for our customers and for us.

These changes let us develop a pricing strategy based upon *service differentiation.* For years, we had continually lowered our freight rates, but cost rose to the point of no profitability. We were becoming a commodity business—definitely not where we wanted to be. So we changed our methods by offering better service to customers at a higher price, yet still below what they would pay to ship by truck.

It was a huge change of mindset. Our salespeople wanted lower prices to get business, but instead they had to get it by offering the best service. Had we simply increased price, we would have lost customers. But with improved service and reliability, customers were willing to pay more. When their goods were delivered faster and more reliably, it benefited their business.

Sharing with Our Suppliers

As we improved our business practices and raised our standards, we required our contractors to improve, too. Martita Mullen, Project Manager in charge of upgrading our Memphis terminal, tells this story:

> I'm normally a pretty calm person—but there are limits to everything.
>
> Upgrading and conversion of the Memphis terminal involved reconstruction of the Johnston Switchyard. A critical step in this process was installation of two new switches. To speed this process, we contracted the changeover.
>
> The morning of the change came and I was ready to go. It seems, however, that I was the only one. The contractor chosen

for the assignment had dropped just about every ball he could. Their tamper, a critical tool in stabilizing the rail bed for the new switch, had not been calibrated. Their ballast regulator was leaking hydraulic fluid, and eventually it was decided that it couldn't be used that day.

Their trackmobile was six miles away instead of being on-site where needed. You might not know a lot about trackmobiles, so I'll give you a key statistic—they travel at about three miles an hour on the road. Another two-hour delay.

Each one of these screw-ups was a crime against productivity and common sense. However, the biggest insult was that the contractor knew about these issues, and instead of calling a day or two before, they thought they could muddle through and we wouldn't notice.

But the day wasn't over! A lot of passionate phone calls came from my cell over the next few hours to get things moving. Nevertheless, it still took until 4:00 P.M. before their tamper was ready. Their employees didn't seem to care. They said the holidays were coming up and they could use the overtime. What a way to run a business!

Finally, the equipment was there, the laborers were in place, and they were ready to cut the track. The only thing missing was their equipment operator. . . .

We can skip that part of the story. Let's just say their foreman ran the machine.

We had started the day at 7:00 A.M. and finished at 11:00 P.M. and changed only one of the two switches. With a CN crew, it would have been two switches in eight hours and even then Hunter would have said we were having a relaxed day!

I knew one thing after that day: It wasn't only the track that was going to get switched.[1]

Experiences like that were persuasive: If we need something critical done, we do it ourselves. That way, we build internal expertise, keep our people working, and maintain control.

We're not done making demands on suppliers. As Hunter said, "We are willing to pay top dollar for their services, but they must be willing to do what they say they will do."

For example, to keep our service competitive, and get the price for it, we will need faster trains. That requires dramatic improvement in equipment reliability. We will be looking for our suppliers to meet this challenge.

Sharing with Our Competitors

It may sound counterintuitive to welcome competition, but we do in the railroad industry. The stronger the rail industry, the more we all benefit, because a stronger rail industry attracts more rail customers. Then it's up to us to differentiate CN's services from competing rail lines.

Our main competitor in Canada has a similar view:

> CN has the lowest operating ratio [of any railway] in North America. CN's main rival in the north, Canadian Pacific Railway, Ltd., has reduced its operating ratio. But that is not enough for CP's chief executive, who encouraged other rail lines to follow CN's lead, like his company has.
>
> "We're at a point where CN was a number of years ago. I'm not proud. To the extent we can steal all of their best ideas and implement them, we shall do that as fast as we possibly can."
>
> He went on to say, "There should be a collective objective in the rail industry to close the efficiency gap with CN."[2]

We're all for closing that efficiency gap. The more our competitors close it, the more we're pushed to open it further ahead. We've worked on several ways to share with our competitors:

- CN started an annual Human Resources/Labor Relations conference that includes competing railroads. We all agreed on recruiting, testing, and screening protocols, and designed common training programs. These programs saved us all time and money.
- We developed a benefits and compensation survey and run it annually.

- CN's executive assessment program has been duplicated by other railroads.
- This sharing of best practices has been duplicated elsewhere in CN, including our departments of IT, Finance, and Transportation.
- We invite competitors to attend Hunter Camp. We make no secret of the camp's content, and we give Hunter's book, *How We Work and Why*, to everyone who attends—including competitors.

We are not giving away our commercially sensitive information on proprietary secrets. CN is successful not because of what's in the book or the camps. CN is successful because our leaders know how to execute and our employees know how to deliver.

Sharing with Our Communities

We play a significant role in the communities we serve. We are a major employer, a service company to other employers, and a neighbor to residents.

In our multiple roles, we feel a responsibility to support the communities we live and work in. That support takes many shapes. The following example is just one way we have worked to strengthen our communities.

> With a purposeful double-barreled focus on schools and enforcement, Chief Inspector Dan Ritchie and his CN police force in British Columbia have successfully reduced the number of incidents at rail crossings throughout the province by 33 percent in 2005 compared to 2004. This exceptional effort has propelled the force to number one status among all CN police divisions.
>
> They write more tickets, catch more trespassers, and close more breaking-and-entering cases than any other division in the CN network. How does the B.C. division statistically stay head-and-shoulders above the rest? This is their story.

Dan called his entire team together early in the year for a group brainstorming on how they could impact the number of incidents at rail crossings (involving trains and autos) and trespassers (hit by trains) in their area of responsibility. They zeroed in on two ideas that they believed would make a tremendous impact:

1. Ensure each officer does a minimum of six school safety talks a year—with a focus on schools close to mainline train runs.
2. Increase enforcement efforts in those areas (e.g., increase the number of traffic tickets issued). In 2004, officers charged 1,200 drivers at rail crossings throughout British Columbia (a significant number—more than any of the other provinces). For 2005, Dan's enforcement-focused people wanted to ensure that they did more. The total for 2005 exceeded 1,800.

"We've taken a zero tolerance policy to trespassing," Dan said. "We've charged 487 trespassers so far this year." Last year's total was 300, in itself an unbelievable number compared to years past. (The next-closest province did 200.)

Also in 2005, the British Columbia division ran more than 80 joint-forces operations aimed at the crossing and trespassing safety programs.

Through the process, Dan provided his officers with a lot of positive reinforcement and with the tools they need to complete their objectives. He met quarterly with each person to track how they were doing.

During these one-hour sessions, Dan used the DCOM® model (Direction, Competence, Opportunity, Motivation) to determine if there was anything he could do to help officers meet their collective goals.

"Using the tools taught in the ABC process makes so much sense," Dan said. "My guys are already doing a wonderful job, but we can do more."

Dan summarizes the experience: "As a group, they developed the strategy to limit the number of incidents due to trespassing—with phenomenal results. All of their hard work at crossings, in schools, in rail yards, and elsewhere has dramatically improved safety in British Columbia."

In the end, change that strengthens CN has the potential to make things better for our customers, suppliers, communities, and the rail industry as a whole. Change alters everything.

31

Improving Relations with Our Unions

CN is 80 percent unionized, with about 20 unions and 100 collective agreements representing 18,000 employees company-wide. We experienced two strikes in four years—with the Canadian Auto Workers in 2004 (described in Chapter 14) and the United Transportation Union in 2007. We sought neither strike.

In the discipline of labor relations, we work at getting to yes instead of walking out. Finding solutions through conversation, not conflict, builds the best foundation for culture change. These strikes were switchpoints in our culture change.

The 2007 UTU Strike

In 2007, our conductors, represented by the United Transportation Union (UTU), walked out. During negotiations that led to the strike, the UTU leadership pressed for wage and benefit increases far beyond the railway industry pattern we had established. With hours left before the strike deadline, the union still had almost a hundred issues left to be addressed. Although we offered multiple alternatives to resolve the dispute, each met with a firm *no*.

A union's power to strike is its ultimate form of leverage, since it slows or halts the company's operations. The UTU leadership was likely thinking that we wouldn't risk a strike in winter weather, when experienced workers are most needed. In the past decade,

CN's bargaining team, in some minds, had blinked and given in to demands to avoid strikes.

But we couldn't afford to blink. CN stands behind what it says, and our message consistently has been: We can do better together or face the status quo together.

Improved compensation packages need to correspond to improvements in the way we operate. We have worked successfully with many of our union groups to rewrite our agreements to provide superior compensation and quality of life to our employees (the union members) in exchange for productivity improvements.

Despite our success with most of our union groups, we had yet to make the breakthrough with the running trades (engineers, conductors, and trainmen) in Canada. So, with no agreement at the strike deadline, the UTU walked out during one of the harshest winters in years.

To replace our 2,500 striking conductors, we trained 600 CN managers to be conductors. A conductor is responsible for enforcing operating procedures and directing a train's crew.

Managers who took on service jobs during the Canadian Auto Workers strike in 2004 were trained to run engines and switch cars. They made a smooth transition into an area that was foreign to them. They learned how to work as a team in a completely different setting.

It gave our managers a firsthand look at what our unionized employees do daily, giving them a better understanding of tasks in unionized jobs. They learned what it was like to keep the railroad operating physically, and this made them better railroaders.

The engineers who run our trains stayed on the job (they work under a different union agreement) and worked alongside our management replacements. We reduced service but kept running trains.

To the disbelief of industry observers, our management conductors did well. In wintry conditions only a polar bear could love, they faced one operating challenge after another in sub-zero temperatures, ice, and blinding snow. They pulled together and formed a close-knit team.

CN is part of the transportation backbone of Canada, so a very interested observer of the strike was the Canadian government. When the CAW had struck CN (Chapter 14), we had settled that dispute without assistance. So Ottawa watched and waited. As weeks slipped by, goods like grain and lumber moved in smaller volumes than before the strike, and protests from our customers rose. Finally, the government enacted back-to-work legislation.

Conductors were back on the job and managers returned to their offices. We went through government-mandated arbitration. After months of controversy, the arbitrator imposed the wage-and-benefit package we submitted, which was comparable to the package we offered before the strike deadline.

When to Say Yes, When to Say No

There was a humbling aspect of both the CAW and UTU strikes. We realized that some conflicts could be avoided if managers paid more attention to employees' needs. With the command-and-control management culture we had in the past, we had sometimes overlooked the basic need to stay tuned in to our employees.

The strikes reminded managers that CN's employees work hard, and often under difficult conditions. Saying yes to basic requests whenever possible was simply the right thing to do, and it made employees feel good about the company.

Saying no can be the right answer, too.

In collective bargaining, both the company and its employees must be prepared to give and take. The company and unions often will agree on some issues and their solutions. But there are times when the company or the union must say no. The key is to understand *why* one party is saying no, and to seek a better solution.

"You have to come prepared to say no, and walk away when you know it's the right thing to do," Hunter says. "The best way to say no is to explain why, and let reason prevail rather than anger."

We increased our communication with employees before, during, and after both strikes. We wanted them to be clear on the value proposition of our offer and be able to weigh the options when they voted.

Today, we send a monthly message to all employees, updating them on "people services." The more our people know, the better choices they can make.

Confronting a Long Legacy

Negotiations in the rail industry often focus on the past, particularly when one party or the other is seeking to change the status quo.

Grievances about past conduct are like ghosts: They can haunt the future and become a rallying cry.

Our UTU agreements in the U.S. are not based on how we run trains today. They are based on laws and the way we ran trains with steam engines a century ago. We don't talk about an "hour's pay" as you might expect. Instead, we talk of pay in terms of distance: "12½ miles." That made sense 80 years ago: A steam engine could run about 100 miles in an eight-hour day, so an hour was worth about 12½ miles.

After almost 100 years of operating experience, we had thought of ways to change that system to the benefit of all concerned. So in the 2007 UTU negotiations, one of our alternative packages offered the union and employees a new way of thinking about train operations and employee compensation.

But rather than take the leap of faith to consider how to make this concept work in Canada, the UTU leaders found reasons to oppose this thinking. In some union leaders' minds, we had not successfully managed our operations under the old system. If we could not do that, they said, how could they risk changing the rules in some dramatic way?

In the end, both parties lost because we had not dealt with the problems from the past. We ended up with an imposed status quo deal. We learned from this experience, and in the future will explain the how and why of our ideas in better detail.

Change is a must-do for CN—we can't give up on it. Our strikes taught us a big lesson about the need to change culture. To move into the future, we have to get the past behind us.

We have to show employees that change is good for them as well as for the company. The only way to do so is to share the benefits of change.

After the 2007 UTU strike, the local union leadership was removed and a union merger was in the works. CN hopes the new union leadership looks to the future and will be willing to discuss ideas about change that will result in financial benefit to employees. When employees clearly see the benefits of change, they are less resistant to it.

Did we handle it perfectly? No. If we had, we would have avoided a strike and come to an agreement that met our mutual needs, an agreement that kept the company moving forward. However, we learned a lot about ourselves as leaders, the challenges we still face, and just how tough it is to change over 100 years of history.

The United Steelworkers

Since CN's privatization in 1995, we have accelerated the speed of culture change, not only in how we manage people, but in how we negotiate collective agreements. We are unafraid to say no, even when facing a strike, if the cost of avoiding the strike is to compromise our principles and the behaviors we are trying to change.

This doesn't mean we are reluctant to work with our union leaders—quite the opposite. Leo Gerard International President of the United Steelworkers (USW), and Ken Neumann, USW National Director for Canada, are representative of union leaders who are looking at how to position their unions for the future while living in today's business environment.

Our first exposure to these leaders was at a meeting to discuss safety issues following a derailment. As one observer noted, the meeting was classic labor relations at its finest. Hunter led CN's team and Leo led the USW team in a discussion of critical issues. Their collective skill in expressing their positions, at times passionately, was equal only to their skill in defusing a tense discussion.

The meeting could have ended with a fist fight, but in the hands of these veteran deal makers we all walked away with clear direction and a commitment to better understand each other's needs. That commitment led to other meetings, and a true mutual respect grew between these leaders.

Like the USW, most of our unions have listened to our message, and have understood that they succeed when the railway succeeds. For example, as a result of our frequent discussions, the USW leadership has been a leader in translating CN's vision into better working agreements for its membership. When Hunter explained to our union leaders that he would pay for productivity, Leo Gerard and Ken Neumann asked, "How much and for what?" As a result, for the past two rounds of bargaining, the USW has negotiated longer-term agreements with productivity improvements and wage and benefit improvements in excess of other unions on our properties.

Importantly, these agreements have been negotiated directly between the parties without federal assistance or strike threat. It's the way we like to do business with our partners.

Leo and Ken understood our message that we needed to change together. As the steel industry reorganized, they saw what happened to an industry that refused to keep pace with market demands. They understood that our employees' time and work are like investments in the success of the company, and that if the contracts they negotiate result in improved productivity, their members should receive a return on their investment in terms of wages and/ or job security.

Their curiosity about how we operate our business and their dedication to meet with our senior leadership routinely to understand our business direction helped us reposition our relationship with the group of employees represented by their union.

Improving Labor Relations

Despite the goodwill and improved relations, we still experienced two strikes in the past four years with the CAW and UTU, as previously described.

In the CAW strike, we all assumed too much. We had reached a good agreement with their bargaining committee, and they had sent an endorsement to their membership, expecting employees to accept their recommendation.

The CAW is one of Canada's most powerful unions. It was unheard of that employees would reject a tentative agreement that had been endorsed by the entire CAW bargaining committee.

Yet they did, because many of the employees did not even vote on the tentative agreement. This "silent majority" allowed those employees who were unhappy about our culture change to vote down the agreement by a slim margin. We understand that almost 70 percent of our employees either voted for the agreement or didn't act, so the unhappy 30 percent drove a month-long strike. We all learned from that experience.

In 2006, with the contract up for renewal, both sides did much better at listening to and educating the workforce. We dedicated time to local grievance handling, and we increased communication before, during, and after negotiations.

One of the most significant changes, however, was the personal involvement of top leaders from both CN and the union. Hunter and the CAW's Buzz Hargrove were at the table several times during the six months of bargaining. This set the tone and objectives going forward. Their personal attention to the relationship told our employees and managers that we all were moving forward together.

All our efforts paid off. We again negotiated a good agreement, this time ratified by almost 80 percent of employees. Our union leadership and our employees better understood where we were going and why. Their decision to work with us resulted in an agreement that has improved morale, productivity, and job security—a win-win for all.

What CN Brings to the Bargaining Table

When we go to the table, we focus on finding mutually beneficial solutions. We do four things to achieve this:

1. *Look for the win/win solution.* We know what we need to achieve. We have a plan to get there before we start to negotiate. We also plan exit strategies, so we don't back our union colleagues into a corner. We present alternatives long before strike deadlines, so each side can choose options that provide wins for each constituency.
2. *Accept that unions are our partners.* Employees may switch unions, but it is rare that they elect to completely leave union representation. So unionized employees will continue to be a part of our operations. We must accept each other as partners and work together to change the culture.
3. *Know that culture change takes time.* Culture change happens one employee at a time. No matter how good a contract we negotiate with the union leadership, it is useless unless every employee and manager understands the *why* of each negotiated change. Our negotiated agreements and management practices have to work in tandem to reward our employees collectively and individually.
4. *Remember that today's strike is tomorrow's legacy.* It would have been easier to accept the union's demands and avert the conductors' strike. But to change the culture and manage expectations for the future, we couldn't afford that. When we tell employees, "You must do what you say you are going to do," we also must be willing to stand squarely behind our best offers. Our successors will reap the benefits of our decisions for years to come.

CN prides itself on being a company of great railroaders. The principles by which we run our business apply as much to our employees and their unions as to our customers or suppliers. Hunter has reminded us often that we must say no to any demand that conflicts with our vision and direction.

All union leaders with whom we deal want CN to prosper and succeed—as they say, a successful CN can afford higher wages, better benefits, and greater job security. While our union and management teams may sometimes differ on the means, we almost always agree on what the end should be: a fair contract that allows both company and employees to continue outperforming our competitors.

The Future

As Hunter stated in his prestrike letter to the CAW, "Unfortunately, as we know from watching past strikes in the railroad industry, nobody wins, and our relationship will be damaged for a long time." Employees lose, customers lose, and CN's shareholders lose.

The first decade of the twenty-first century has seen CN and its unions take big steps toward a new culture of understanding and cooperation. We hope this sets the tone for the future as CN grows.

PART VIII

LEARNING FROM OUR JOURNEY

We understand that this will not be the last time we undertake significant cultural change! This is an ongoing, multiyear effort to keep the company moving in the right direction. To help drive change faster in the future, we took time to take stock of the learnings we had experienced, so we could replicate the successes and avoid the failures in the future.

CHAPTER

32

Top 10 Tips for Leaders Using the ABC Methodology

To fill the need we saw, we developed the following top 10 tips for leaders to use the ABC methodology effectively. In this chapter, we discuss in detail each of these tips.

Tip 1: Manage Your Culture

Everyone's behavior (what you say and do) is directly influenced by your supervisor, whether you are the CEO or a first-line employee. Your supervisor determines what you are expected to do (job performance) and what the reward will be (consequences). Your performance is directly related to how you are managed.

Every day, you set standards, communicate, measure, and create consequences for people, and that determines your workplace's culture and performance. Most of how your organization feels comes from you and the people around you. You must manage your culture.

A living example: A major employer in our headquarters' city was in bankruptcy, and resumes from their unhappy employees were flowing into CN. But one department in this company yielded not a single resume. We discovered that the department leader was a master of culture, able to motivate, engage, and inspire his people despite the bankruptcy. His people trusted his leadership and he sustained a want-to workplace even in hard times.

Tip 2: Measure What You Value

As long as people know what's expected, why, and what's in it for them, 90 to 95 percent of employees will proudly do their jobs well.

Do your employees know what your company values? If you have too many priorities, or they conflict, or are unclearly stated, employees become confused and unfocused. They can't understand the priorities.

Not having this clear direction is a top complaint at most companies. Keep your priorities to five or six. Specifically define good, better, and best results. Explain what and why with total clarity. Then measure peoples' performance on your priorities.

Tip 3: Challenge, Disagree, and Then Make the Decision

We are all professionals, and we won't agree 100 percent of the time. So it is essential to tap everyone's ideas.

Difference of opinion is good: It gives everyone an opportunity to have their say, it makes discussions real, it makes decisions more likely to be right, and it generates buy-in.

Once the decision is made, support it and the leader who made it.

Tip 4: Focus on Behavior You See or Hear at Work

If an employee does not behave (perform) to expectations, you need to work at how you are managing this employee. To do this, you have to act on what *you observe at work, what you see and hear.*

It's tempting to relate an individual's personal life to his job performance. Despite your good intentions, most of the time you will get it wrong. Most people who are engaged in their work keep personal issues from affecting their performance.

Tip 5: Ask "Would You, If Your Life Depended on It?"

Behavior is influenced by antecedents (less than 20 percent) and by consequences (80 percent or greater). Consequences have by far the greater impact on employees' behavior.

Some have difficulty believing that 80 percent of performance is due to motivation that is driven by consequences. So think about it this way: If someone is not performing at the expected level, do you think they would do it *if their life depended on it?* If you answer yes, then the issue is motivation/consequences.

Tip 6: Transition from Good to Great Performers

The difference between a good team and a great team is the leader's ability to motivate—to apply positive consequences.

The best way is through engagement, commitment, and the resulting pride of the team members. Pride is an incredible driver of Discretionary Performance[SM].

Tip 7: Deal Quickly with Poor Performers

Many managers err by not dealing early with performance issues.

They want to avoid conflict or awkwardness and hope the situation will improve on its own. Often, this ends in a blowup because the manager has finally had enough. This is a complete lose-lose for the person with the performance problem, the co-workers, the supervisor, and the whole company.

By acting early, you can guide most people back to standards you expect, through coaching and restating your expectations. DCOM® and pinpointing will help you get at the issue. Then you can use consequences to change their performance.

Tip 8: Get Face-to-Face

Talking one-on-one, eyeball-to-eyeball, is the most effective way to influence someone.

If you receive positive feedback from your leader in person, it's very satisfying. The strongest way for leaders to thank employees for their hard work is a simple handshake and smile.

The same is true when you need to confront someone's poor performance. They can't avoid the issue when you are eyeball-to-eyeball with them.

Tip 9: Balance Your Use of Consequences

The three types of feedback are positive, constructive, and none at all. These need to be balanced.

To build a positive relationship over time, provide on average about four positive consequences (like praise) for each constructive consequence. To be effective, the ratio of positive feedback to constructive feedback must be at least four to one. It's important to know your people, because each individual has his own balance of consequences.

No consequence at all equates to "death by indifference." When you provide no consequence, you leave it up to the individual to guess what you think. This is bad for morale and it is poor leadership—don't do it.

Tip 10: Manage the Learning Curve

Manage the learning curve or it will manage you.

Intelligent, aggressive extroverts can appear to be further along than they are, and they often believe it themselves. But a green, overconfident employee can make serious mistakes—and mistakes can be fatal on the railroad.

Be careful not to put people into roles beyond what they are ready for. We want them to stretch, not break.

Once you properly pace an employee to be fully skilled and confident, your role changes from basic instruction to coaching for even higher performance.

33

The Culture Change
We Achieved

Overall, we have made great strides in improving our leadership. The rollout of the Five Guiding Principles was started with the book *How We Work and Why*, reinforced through the ABC workshops, and supported by the Employee Performance Scorecard (EPS) process. Most employees can articulate the Five Guiding Principles and describe how their jobs fit into each one.

The second layer—leaders using the Twelve Characteristics of Leadership—was achieved through the Hunter Camp experience and the ABC training. The continuous performance improvement mind-set across CN is evolving, and in some cases it is being accelerated through new employee orientation. The sense of pride and professionalism is being enhanced through our Railroader Certification process.

Do we have every employee more involved and engaged? The answer is yes for about 85 percent of our employees. There is still room to grow, but great progress has already been achieved.

Ten Lessons Learned from Our Switchpoints

Throughout our journey, we have used many tools, techniques, and ideas to continue to develop the organization's culture. Looking back, 10 things were absolutely critical to our success.

Lesson 1: Clarity in vision. The vision was clear—continue to be the leading railroad in North America, and do this through leading effectively with the Five Guiding Principles.

Lesson 2: Commitment to change by both the CEO and leadership team. The leadership team was committed, engaged, and actively sponsoring the cultural change. Without their sponsorship, we could not have made the progress we did.

Lesson 3: A proven leadership methodology. Anchoring our culture change on the ABC methodology allowed us consistency in what our leaders needed to do to change, and gave them a process to use in determining why employees are, or aren't, engaging in the need for our desired change.

Lesson 4: Developmental opportunities. Along the way, we created developmental opportunities to offer support and training to leaders and employees who were trying to move from the old culture to the new (such as the certificate programs, Railroad MBA, Hunter Camps, etc.).

Lesson 5: Results focus. While we worked to change the organization's culture (pattern of behaviors), we always did it in a way that would further improve our business results. Changing behaviors just to make a change would not be sustainable.

Lesson 6: Communication. We developed several vehicles to communicate the vision, cultural change success stories, progress against goals, and other key messages to the organization.

Lesson 7: Customization. We developed a centralized, core curriculum that was deployed regionally. That deployment relied heavily on customizing the core content to best meet the needs of the region by using the tools to address their most critical issues.

Lesson 8: Information and accountability. As the culture shifted, we shared more information with leaders at all levels of the organization. Their roles developed into stronger decision-making roles, and they were held accountable for making decisions appropriate to their role.

Lesson 9: Staggered rollout. We carefully planned the rollout of the culture change to meet the largest yards first, followed by the smaller, more rural yards. This rollout plan gave us great flexibility and the opportunity to gain support for changes before going organization-wide.

Lesson 10: Horizontal and vertical alignment. We started driving vertical alignment through the regions. Then, as the need arose, we worked to develop horizontal alignment across multiple functions in the organization. This let us improve communications, work processes, and individual relationships.

CHAPTER

34

The Final Word

Books about corporate culture are by necessity snapshots. If the authors are true to their task, such books present a fair portrait up to the present—which in this book means early 2008. But what such books are stunningly bad at is predicting what the future will look like.

For example, if you were to read an old book about the 3M Company, it would be about the mining of ores by the Minnesota Mining and Manufacturing Company (hence the name 3M). It wouldn't foretell a future of Post-it® notes, Scotch® tape, and 75,000 other products.

Similarly, this book has focused on a snapshot in CN's history—our remarkable transformation during 2003 through 2007.

The Transformation

As we said earlier, in the railway business, there is no secret technological edge. There is no machine or patent that conveys to CN its success. Every engine, piece of track, and machine that CN owns is duplicated in the inventories of its competitors.

Thus, what CN has achieved during the period from Paul Tellier's arrival in 1992, through Hunter Harrison's joining the organization in 1998 and becoming CEO in 2003, and up to today, has been done strictly through the performance of people. Success is defined by the way we lead and the way we execute.

Our actions—that is, our behaviors—delivered dramatic improvements in our results. Between 2003 and 2007, CN's stock outperformed all major North American stock indices. In addition to stock performance, we also showed improvements in all key metrics from 2002 to 2006:

- Free cash flow increased 162 percent (from $513 million to $1.343 billion).
- Revenue improved 25 percent (from $6.339 billion to $7.929 billion).
- Net income rose 72 percent (from $1.052 billion to $1.81 billion).
- Operating ratio dropped significantly (from 70.5 to 61.8 percent).

These improvements earned CN the distinction of being the best-running railroad in North America.

What Lies Ahead

Looking back is easy. Predicting what CN will be like in the future is difficult. We can foresee many factors that will challenge and change us:

- *Increasing competition from all quarters.* Any time an organization is continuously successful, like CN, someone will emulate it and try to better it. That is the downside of being on top in your industry. If CN doesn't advance, the world will advance around us. To remain leading and profitable, CN must continue to change, finding ways to maintain and increase our value to our customers.
- *The environment in which we operate.* Our last decade of operation has seen too many once-in-a-lifetime weather events to think that the future won't be equally challenging.
- *The economy.* This endless challenge to all organizations is a lesson history visits on the world every time we think we've got it all worked out.
- *The increasing average age of the population.* Like a long train in the distance, the slow population shift has tricked many organizations. It can be seen in the distance, gradually moving closer for quite a while, and it doesn't appear to be moving that

quickly, but suddenly it thunders into view. This will accelerate culture change at CN.

These known obstacles are significant, but they aren't the only things we need to think about. If history has shown us anything, it is that known obstacles are not half of what is to come.

Our goals of expanding the scope of CN to a worldwide transportation company and continuously improving performance and profitability are audacious—some would even say a dream. But what we have achieved today was all a dream just 20 years ago, as CN sat in last place, the worst railway in North America.

Today, CN is one of the top railroads in North America. The key to attaining our future goals will be to learn from our failures and build on our successes.

Where We Are Now

To meet these challenges of the future, CN will rely on the key element of our past success—our people. In this area, the journey is far from over. Even with our successes, there have been setbacks and challenges, and there is still much opportunity ahead.

The risk is that culture change can be fragile if not tended to correctly. Reward the wrong behaviors, fail to recognize the right ones, be unclear on expectations, and the behaviors you get—the sum of which is your culture—will not be the culture you wanted, or the one that will help your company and employees prosper in the future.

It is CN's leaders and our employees who will either enhance or detract from what we have achieved. With a good understanding of our principles, our business, and the models we use to lead, they will be able to use their own unique knowledge and life experiences to build on the culture we have created. It will make all the difference.

If you look at our progress to date using the Organizational Culture Continuum, you can see how far CN has come. (See Figure 34.1.)

Some might ask, "Are you frustrated that the entire organization has not progressed to 'engaged' yet?" Not in the least. We knew this would be a long journey, with large steps forward and small steps back. Lasting change through a company of this size takes time and hard work to ensure consistency.

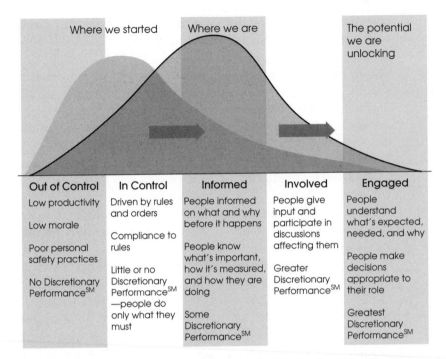

Out of Control	In Control	Informed	Involved	Engaged
Low productivity	Driven by rules and orders	People informed on what and why before it happens	People give input and participate in discussions affecting them	People understand what's expected, needed, and why
Low morale	Compliance to rules	People know what's important, how it's measured, and how they are doing	Greater Discretionary Performance^{SM}	People make decisions appropriate to their role
Poor personal safety practices	Little or no Discretionary Performance^{SM} —people do only what they must			
No Discretionary Performance^{SM}		Some Discretionary Performance^{SM}		Greatest Discretionary Performance^{SM}

Figure 34.1   CN's Progress on the Organization Culture Continuum
Source: Adapted from materials provided by Peter Edwards.

We have seen the results we can create when leaders choose to lead using Q4 Leadership^{SM}, and when employees are engaged, focused, and committed. We aren't there yet. Across the organization, we have differing levels of leadership—we need to help all leaders move toward Q4.

Even then, our leaders are not yet consistent—sometimes, under pressure, they slip back. We need to determine ways to help them stay the course, even in the roughest times, to ensure continuous improvement.

In the end, that's the only way to stay in the game. Our culture change and the tools we have put in place are all about being in the game for the long term.

The Trip Is Not Over

The same trip plan and tools used to drive our past success will allow us to be successful in the future. By revisiting the seven steps of our trip plan, we will be able to adjust and adapt as we need to.

1. *Clarify the vision.* Living the vision means ensuring that everyone across the company always understands it and continues to live the Five Guiding Principles.

2. *Choose the right switchpoints.* With the vision set and a clear understanding of what we want our culture to be, we are on our way. As we continue to improve and develop, we need to be watchful for switchpoints that will continue to lead us down the right track to lasting culture change.

3. *Select the tools for change.* CN's Five Guiding Principles and CLG's models (ABCs, DCOM®, Q4 Leadership℠, Discretionary Performance℠) are all part of creating an integrated framework for leading and a common culture in which to operate. Process improvement is often seen as the best option. While we did get results that way in the past, it was not until we applied behavioral science that we got deep, fundamental improvements in operations. As we progress into the future, these tools will remain at the core of all that we do.

4. *Align the switches.* We cannot be complacent in believing that we have completely lined the switches to drive culture change. To continue improving, we must be alert for ways to revisit alignment and ensure that all the right switches stay aligned toward our vision of the future.

5. *Assess switchpoint impact.* We have seen many early successes. We have also seen some of our leaders' best intentions backfire, with unintended impacts. As we move forward, it will be important to assess the impact of future switchpoints. We need to track our progress to determine whether we make the right decisions at key switchpoints to stay the course toward our vision of the future.

6. *Spike the switch.* As we align new switches, making decisions to move the company closer to our desired future state, we need to spike the switch to ensure that the culture will continue forward and not fall back into old habits.

7. *Learn from the process.* To continue to improve, we will regularly review the learnings we experience so we can replicate successes and avoid failures in the future.

We have a proven process for culture change that drives results. By creating this common language and culture, we understand each other better and consequently are able to respond faster to our dynamic environment. Through coaching better, we will be a better team. And through engaging, recognizing, and liberating the talents of CN's employees, we will create a force of unlimited creativity and potential.

The hardest challenge for some is to recognize that it is often the little things, done with great care and discipline, that produce the greatest results. Too often they are looking for the trick or the latest fad. The tools we have chosen look simple. Their power comes only in the way people choose to use them.

In the end, it is those choices that will write our future.

Notes

Preface

1. *National Post*, "He Loves That Loonie," February 7, 2008. Material printed with the express permission of: "The National Post Company," a Canwest Partnership.

Chapter 1—The Road to Best-in-Class

1. Quoted from p. 27 in *The Pig That Flew*, by Harry Bruce, published 1997 by Douglas & McIntyre Ltd. Reprinted by permission of the publisher. This veteran journalist's short book is a highly readable account of the Canadian National Railway's IPO.
2. Ibid., p. 154.
3. Ibid.
4. Adapted with permission from E. Hunter Harrison, *Change, Leadership, Mud and Why* (Canadian National Railway Company, 2008).

Chapter 26—Hunter Camps Develop Leaders

1. Morris Massey's contribution is presented in E. Hunter Harrison, *Change, Leadership, Mud and Why* (Canadian National Railway Company, 2008).

Chapter 30—Sharing Our Story

1. Adapted with permission from E. Hunter Harrison, *Change, Leadership, Mud and Why* (Canadian National Railway Company, 2008).
2. *National Post*, "Railways Aim for Peak Efficiency To Meet Demand; Would Help Fight Truckers," May 9, 2007, Financial Post. p. FP 5. Material reprinted with the espress permission of: "The National Post Company," a Canwest Partnership.

About the Authors

SwitchPoints' authors are the people who lived the story and made it breathe.

Judy Johnson, a CLG Partner, applies behavioral science expertise to help leaders create environments that dramatically improve organizational performance and profitability. She also coaches leaders at C level, VP level, and operations level to execute strategy through pinpointing key behaviors that lead to success. She helps improve executive skills in communication, feedback delivery, and decision making.

Johnson's clients span many industries: transportation, pharmaceuticals, financial services, telecommunications, consumer products, manufacturing, petrochemicals, technology, engineering, shipping logistics, and retail services. She has helped organizations realize measurable improvements in customer satisfaction, quality assurance, and traditional performance indicators (revenue growth, safety, customer retention, productivity).

In CN's strongly union environment, Johnson personally coached several key VPs through the multiyear culture change presented in *SwitchPoints.* She managed a team of 20 consultants supporting leaders across the organization. This work sharply improved the company's performance in safety, timeliness, asset utilization, profitability, and shareholder value. She developed 80 internal consultants to support the culture change following CLG's engagement.

Johnson holds a Ph.D. in Applied Behavior Analysis from Western Michigan University (emphasis: Industrial and Organizational Psychology), a Master's in Industrial and Organizational Psychology, a Bachelor's in Psychology and Management, and an MBA Essentials certificate from the University of Pittsburgh's Graduate School of Business.

She has taught university courses in Applied Behavior Analysis and conducted research on feedback, motivation, and productivity. Her published articles and presentations focus on improving performance through feedback, teaming, and incentives.

Les Dakens emphasizes his partnership with CN's CEO Hunter Harrison in steering the corporation where few large organizations have had the courage to venture: implementing behaviorally guided cultural changes, CN's Five Guiding Principles, an Employee Performance System scorecard, and aggressive leadership.

Dakens has successfully aligned CN's people strategy with Harrison's long-term business plans. This extraordinary partnership deserves credit for CN's amazing cultural turnaround and business performance.

Dakens, now retired, was responsible for strategic direction of all aspects of CN's Human Resources and Labor Relations in North America and worldwide. He helped revolutionize how the rail industry works with unions in collective agreements. He managed Labor Relations through two major strikes, an important part of the culture change at CN, and continued to manage HR/LR through challenging demographic shifts in the workforce—for example, one of Canada's largest pension plans for older employees, and a portable plan for younger employees.

Dakens came to this role from the North American division of H. J. Heinz Company, where he was VP of HR. His decade there focused on leadership development and executive assessment for 35 manufacturing facilities in the United States and Canada, working with multiple unions. It was at Heinz that Dakens first worked with CLG, enabling him to introduce CLG's behavioral services at CN.

Dakens is an accomplished HR systems designer, labor negotiator, and co-author of three books.

Peter Edwards' contributions to this book are based on his years of responsibility for human resources, culture change, implementation, leadership, and organizational development for CN in North America. Edwards' recent innovations across CN include:

- Creation and deployment of an Employee Performance Review System (EPS) for CN's 18,500 unionized employees, part of the company's cultural change/performance shift strategy.
- Co-authoring and managing an integrated internal rollout of *Change, Leadership, Mud and Why,* CN's second book on

change and leadership for the company, its suppliers, and the railway industry.

- Development of online Pre-Employment Testing Systems and Management Assessment Centers that have been purchased by other Class I railways.

Edwards helped author CN's first book for employees (*How We Work and Why*), participated in Hunter Camps presented by CN's CEO, and designed CN's Railroad MBA program (all featured in *SwitchPoints*).

Edwards authored the Control to Empowerment model and process for employee culture change currently used in CN's ongoing high-performance transformation. He also introduced Executive Assessment Centers, made available to another Class I railway.

Edwards is implementing online recruitment, employment branding, selection systems, Web-based training, frontline supervisor best practices, a new Performance Management Plan, enhanced succession planning, customer service training, sales training, and sales/customer structure realignment.

He holds a Master's degree in Industrial Relations from Queen's University and has completed executive education in Finance (Wharton School of Business) and Advanced Negotiation and Mediation (Harvard Law School). Edwards is an experienced lecturer, media spokesman, and co-author of three books.

Ned Morse, a CLG Senior Partner, has three decades of experience helping clients execute business-critical strategy more effectively. Working closely with Fortune 50 corporate executives to develop and implement their plans, Morse has helped businesses realize significant and measurable improvements in customer satisfaction, employee commitment, and traditional performance indicators such as costs, revenue growth, cycle time, error rates, and profits.

As a consultant, he has worked with over 100 companies to achieve business performance goals through the transformation of internal work practices and processes, assisted business leaders to improve leadership skills through one-to-one executive coaching, and helped executives align organizational culture with stated values and principles.

Morse has worked with clients in oil and gas, food service, health care, defense, semiconductors, chemicals, engineering, telecommunications, insurance, pharmaceuticals, retail, and manufacturing.

Morse earned his MBA from the Wharton School. Prior to joining CLG, he was a Senior Partner and National Practice Director of Performance Improvement Consulting Services for the Hay Group and VP/Managing Director for Aubrey Daniels & Associates. Morse is an active speaker with more than 300 articles, lectures, and workshops to his credit.

About the Companies

Canadian National Railway

Canadian National Railway (CN) is "North America's Railroad"—the only transcontinental network in North America, serving ports on the Atlantic, Pacific, and Gulf coasts, linking customers to all three NAFTA nations. Ports on all three coasts link CN to clients in Europe and Asia.

CN is a highly competitive leader in rail and intermodal transportation. The company has the rail industry's best operating ratio, best profit margin, strong free cash flow performance, and balance sheet, and has handsomely rewarded its shareholders in the past decade. The company is committed to safely moving more freight, more quickly, using fewer assets, than any other rail line.

CN moves a highly diversified, balanced portfolio of goods, including petroleum and chemicals, grain and fertilizers, coal, metals and minerals, forest products, automobiles and parts, and worldwide intermodal freight.

CLG (The Continuous Learning Group)

CLG is the world's premiere behavioral science consultancy, serving corporations since 1993. The company today has scores of consultants working with Fortune 50, 100, and 500 companies in North America, Europe, Asia, and Australia.

More than a century of research into Applied Behavioral Science has given CLG a deep understanding of human performance. CLG's consultants apply the proven laws of human behavior to business processes and strategies, and through this CLG has become a world leader in behavior-based strategy execution and performance-improvement consulting. CLG's expertise in Applied Behavioral

Science is engaged by clients to implement strategy, improve operations, and develop leadership effectiveness.

CLG's consultants have helped CEOs and senior leaders manage mergers of some of the world's largest corporations. The CLG difference is evident in clients' successes.

Index